WILDCAT MADNESS

GOLDEN
OF COLLEGE SPORTS
AGES

WILDCAT MADNESS

Great Eras in Kentucky Basketball

WILTON SHARPE

CUMBERLAND HOUSE
NASHVILLE, TENNESSEE

WILDCAT MADNESS
PUBLISHED BY CUMBERLAND HOUSE PUBLISHING, INC.
431 Harding Industrial Drive
Nashville, TN 37211-3160

Cover design: Gore Studio, Inc.
Text design: John Mitchell
Research/administrative assistant: Ariel Robinson

Library of Congress Cataloging-in-Publication Data

Sharpe, Wilton.
    Wildcat madness : great eras in Kentucky basketball / Wilton Sharpe.
        p. cm. — (Golden ages of college sports)
    Includes bibliographical references and index.
    ISBN-13: 978-1-58182-473-5 (pbk. : alk. paper)
    ISBN-10: 1-58182-473-4 (pbk. : alk. paper)
    1. Kentucky Wildcats (Basketball team)—History. 2. University of Ken-tucky—Basketball—History. I. Title. II. Series.
    GV885.43.U53S528 2005
    796.323'630976947—dc22

                                                            2005030096

Printed in the United States of America

1 2 3 4 5 6—10 09 08 07 06 05

For Owen,
thank you for being the perfect man
in my little girl's life.
And may True Blue forever line your pathway

and Caroline,
thank you, dearest, for your endless patience,
commitment, and dedication to our love

Ralph Beard

CONTENTS

Introduction   9

1 Origins of Blue   11

2 The Big Blue   29

3 Wildcat Character   45

4 Heroes and Icons   53

5 Legendary Coaches   87

6 Scandal   115

7 Major Moments   127

8 The Kentucky Wildcats
    All-Time Team   153

9 The Great Kentucky Fives   161

10 Royal Courts of Blue   181

11 Winning and Losing   189

12 Bitter Foes   201

13 The Wildcat Faithful   209

14 The Ball Bag   223

15 Kentucky National Champion Rosters   237

    Bibliography   *245*
    Index   *249*

INTRODUCTION

In the fall of 1961, a skinny 17-year-old Connecticut kid heading into his senior season of high school was pulled like a magnet to a college basketball preseason All-America team spotlighted in the pages of *Sport* magazine. The grand old publication at the time was renowned for its magnificent portfolio of Ozzie Sweet full-page color photos.

It gave me my first look at Kentucky basketball in general and the Wildcats' glamorous, blond-haired boy wonder, Cotton Nash, in particular. Elegantly posed shooting a hook shot and already touted as a future great, Nash did not fail to hit the mark while in Lexington. One look at the image of "King Cotton" that day and I was hooked.

It would be hard for even the mildest of college basketball observers not to fall under the mystical spell of Kentucky basketball. The Baron, the sparkling galaxy of stars, the national championships, the tradition, the fans—all interlock into a uniquely fascinating tapestry of heroes and character, headlines and characters.

Wildcat Madness is the story of Big Blue basketball as experienced through the voices of its players, coaches, followers, opponents, and the media.

If you cotton to the color of true blue, this is for you. It's Wildcat all the way.

— W.S.

ORIGINS OF BLUE

T he kids in Kentucky start listening to the games on the radio when they are still being burped on their father's shoulder.

Al McGuire

Late Marquette coach/broadcast analyst

L ike swallows to Capistrano, the national media flock each spring to Lexington to inspect the latest chapter of University of Kentucky basketball history, an irresistible opus of tumult and triumph in which the present is always measured against the past.

Mark Coomes

Louisville Courier-Journal

❋ ❋ ❋

T he tradition is what amazed me, because when you go around the world . . . people talk about Kentucky basketball.

Eddie Sutton

head coach (1986–89)

❋ ❋ ❋

A t Kentucky, basketball is a type of religion, such a fanatical obsession that they expect to be national champions each year, and they live and die with each ball game.

Al McGuire

The late Gov. Happy Chandler counted himself one of Adolph Rupp's best friends and used to sing "My Old Kentucky Home" on Senior Day.

Pat Forde
former writer for the Louisville Courier-Journal/
current ESPN.com college basketball columnist

* * *

They say that a grown man isn't supposed to cry but I couldn't help but let my tears flow when they played "My Old Kentucky Home."

Sam Bowie
center (1980, '81, '84)

* * *

People throughout this state really care about basketball. Businessmen tell me that business goes up and down, depending on whether we win or not. When we lose, a little bit of those people dies.

Joe B. Hall
*former UK assistant coach (1966–72)/
head coach (1973–85)*

EARLY INKLINGS
OF BLUE

The Kentucky Wildcats had a less than sterling beginning when the game of basketball first debuted on the Lexington campus in 1903. In the Big Blue's first eight campaigns, losing seasons were posted seven times, including the first six seasons in a row. But the turnaround to respectability came quickly.

Three years after the school's first winning season (5–4) in 1908–09, Kentucky went undefeated (9–0 in 1912) and was declared Southern champion. It would be 19 seasons before the fabled Rupp era would lift the UK program to exalted heights, but the Wildcats, in a sense preparing for their future greatness under the Baron, recorded 13 winning seasons from 1913 through 1930, with only five negative-balance campaigns.

During that pre-Rupp period, Kentucky displayed its first three All-Americans: forward Basil Hayden (1922), guard Burgess Carey, captain of the 1926 squad, and Carey Spicer, a forward who claimed All-America honors in both 1929 and 1931.

Kentucky demonstrated something new to metropolitan circles. The Southerners, with a background of 29 victories out of their last 30 games and 76 out of there last 85, employ a slow, deliberate style of offense that is built around 13 set plays. . . . It was highly effective.

Louisville Courier-Journal
on the game between Kentucky and NYU in New York City, January 5, 1935—one of only two losses suffered by the SEC co-champion Wildcats that season

⚾ ⚾ ⚾

These four years [1946–49], Kentucky won 128 games and lost nine; it won the National Invitation Tournament when that event was the nation's best; it won the NCAA twice and it helped the United States win the Olympics.

Dave Kindred
author/columnist

THE MAN IN THE BROWN SUIT

A child of the vast plains of Kansas, young Adolph Rupp absorbed the game of basketball like a sponge.

He was fortunate to come under the influence of two of the game's legends—the pioneering founder of basketball, Dr. James A. Naismith, and Dr. Forrest C. "Phog" Allen, illustrious head coach at the University of Kansas and the man regarded as the "father of basketball coaching."

Rupp played on Allen's 1922 national championship team at Kansas, then spent five years as a high school coach before beating out 70 applicants for the UK head coaching job in 1930. His first Kentucky team went 15–3. In just his third season at the Wildcats' helm, Rupp claimed his first SEC Tournament title.

Famous for the brown suit that seemed as much a part of him as his abrasive speech and brusque manner, Rupp fielded four championship teams and one NIT champion (the more prestigious postseason tournament in 1946) in his 42 years as undisputed king of the Bluegrass.

Colorful nicknames helped beatify some of his teams into Kentucky lore: the Fabulous Five, back-to-back NCAA champions of 1948 and '49; the Big Three featured on the undefeated team of 1954, the Fiddlin' Five of '58, and Rupp's Runts, the near-championship team of 1966.

During his lengthy tenure at UK (1930–72), Rupp built a hardwood dynasty that ultimately ran head-on into the face of social change in America. His all-white squads finally met their Waterloo, culminating in the 1966 NCAA championship game against an all-black Texas Western team that roundly thumped Rupp's Runts and loudly signaled the end of all-white sports at major universities in the South.

The point-shaving scandal of the late 1940s-early 1950s, involving six Wildcat players from 1947 through 1950, blackened the eye and cut the legs out from under the great Kentucky program. The school served an unprecedented probation administered jointly by both the NCAA and SEC, with the Wildcats banned from collegiate play for the entire 1952–53 season. But Rupp rebounded with a vengeance. The following season, for the only time in his long career at Kentucky, Rupp's Wildcats went undefeated.

At age 70, Rupp bitterly fought his university-imposed retirement at the conclusion of the 1971–72 season. A dominating, controversial, and colorful chapter in Kentucky basketball annals had none too quietly come to a close.

I've seen all the programs, touching them as a coach, a player, and as an NBC broadcast commentator the past four or five years. I have touched all the so-called capitals of basketball, but when it gets down to the short stroke the only true capital of basketball is Lexington. I even think there are times when the horses kinda bend down a little to the roundball.

Al McGuire

● ● ●

I don't want people here thinking of oil or horses but of Kentucky basketball tickets. I want them to be the most precious thing in life some day.

Rick Pitino
head coach (1990–97)

● ● ●

As theater, Kentucky basketball is sufficiently rousing to engage even one with skeptical predispositions.

Lonnie Wheeler
author

I saw the absolute reverence that the state has for the game of basketball.

Bret Bearup
forward (1981, 1983–85)

● ● ●

Kentucky is an enigmatic corner of the country that, for its own personal, complicated, essentially uncharted reasons, puts a severe provincial spin on an internationally mainstream sport.

Lonnie Wheeler

● ● ●

The tradition of the UK program—it is the winningest in college basketball—obviously contributes to the culture, carrying with it a way-back, ancestral aspect.

Lonnie Wheeler

● ● ●

If you want to survive, you have to have a love for the program.

Joe B. Hall

JOE B. HALL:
FOLLOWING A TOUGH ACT

*T*ry filling the shoes of a deity, one who has had a lengthy run.

Ray Perkins didn't weather the tide at Alabama very long after Paul "Bear" Bryant (also a successful head coach at Kentucky) finally stepped down and into legend, and who remembers John Wooden's successor at UCLA?

That was the unenviable position longtime Kentucky assistant coach Joe B. Hall found himself in as the pretender to the Kentucky throne upon the immortal Rupp's departure prior to the 1972–73 season.

Hall, who once suited up in the Blue and White before transferring to Sewanee to complete his playing career, won the national championship in 1978 and in the process removed the massive weight of post-Rupp expectations. Joe B. went on to record 297 wins in his 13 seasons as Kentucky head coach, second all time behind the Baron.

More importantly, he is credited with integrating the Wildcats program, though Rupp officially gets credit for bringing the first black player to Lexington (7–1 center Tom Payne, in 1969, who turned pro after his sophomore season at UK).

If the school had put a million dollars in my pocket, it wouldn't have meant more to me than that recognition.

Joe B. Hall
on the retirement of his jersey at Rupp Arena,
February 10, 1990

● ● ●

Basketball means just about the same thing in New York and Kentucky. It's just that back home there are lots of other things, and down here it's the only thing.

Jamal Mashburn
forward (1991–93)

● ● ●

For me, it's been a tradition to say we will win right away. These will be exciting years and we want to see something so rich in tradition be brought back the right way.

Rick Pitino

U K has the reputation around the NBA of being the number-one school in the country. Players feel it's even better than UCLA because of Rupp Arena, which . . . is sold out for every game, and because just about the whole state seems to support the team.

Jack Givens
forward (1975–78)

* * *

O ne thing this program needed was a sense of basketball as entertainment.

Rick Pitino

* * *

I think the entire state is overwhelmed by the University of Kentucky.

Wayne Chapman
Rex Chapman's father

FAST EDDIE
AND KENTUCKY'S SHAME

Kentucky's fortunes continued to appear bright after Joe B. Hall retired following the 1985 season. The Wildcats had brought one of the winningest coaches in America to Lexington in Eddie Sutton, the miracle maker at Arkansas, only UK's third head coach since 1930.

Though Sutton guided the Cats to an Elite Eight finish and a fine 32–4 record in his initial season at the Big Blue helm, the grim specter of "Kentucky's Shame," as splattered across the cover of Sports Illustrated in the spring of 1989, wasn't far off.

For the second time in its illustrious history, the Kentucky program was rocked by scandal. The Wildcats were placed on a three-year probation and made to forfeit the SEC regular-season and tournament championships from the 1987–88 season as a consequence of having mailed $1,000 to the father of UK's Chris Mills. What nailed Sutton's coffin shut with finality was the Big Blue's first losing season in over 60 years, a 13–19 mark in 1988–89. Shame, shame. Neither the bellicose Baron nor the demanding Hall had ever registered one of those.

Kentucky basketball, its once-gilded legacy of greatness again besmirched and tarnished, was toppling, a fallen angel.

He's the link between Adolph Rupp and Joe B. Hall, between Kentucky's storied past and it's stirring present.

Billy Reed

sportswriter/author
on longtime Wildcat radio announcer
Cawood Ledford

* * *

My genuine opinion of the Kentucky basketball program is that there is only one and it is top drawer, Park Avenue, and that all other basketball programs in the country think they are, but they are not.

Al McGuire

* * *

Kentucky is the only school anyone cares about.

Anonymous observer

SAVIOR FROM
THE CITY

The blush of "Kentucky's Shame" has been officially replaced by the new flush of Kentucky's fame.
— Mark Coomes
Louisville Courier-Journal, *March 27, 1993,*

● ● ●

Kentucky basketball was at its lowest ebb when Rick Pitino was hired to save the program in 1989. The Wall of Shame had dulled a brighter shade of blue that had reigned regally for over three and a half decades. Well, at least since the last scandal—the point-shaving disgrace of the late '40s.

With his back against the wall, Pitino fought like the streetwise pit bull that he is and, with a skillful blend of talent, diplomacy, guile, and motivation, began to rebuild the championship hopes of the once proud Blue and White.

Though he managed only a 14–14 split his first season in Lexington, Pitino began to reverse the tide near season's end with his team's 100–95 upset win over an LSU squad that featured three future NBA draft choices.

With the burden of sanctions placed on UK by the NCAA in the aftermath of the Sutton-era violations, including scholarship limitations, Pitino still managed to recruit big. He ventured outside the traditional Kentucky mainstream, delving deep into the hotbeds of New York's inner-city playgrounds where he had recruited so successfully in the past, and hit bedrock on which to build his future national championship hopes.

In 1996, after eighteen long years, Kentucky had its sixth national championship and Pitino, in an oddity of cultural blending, was elevated to the status of a Bluegrass demigod.

Pitino even got in on the Name Game, a favorite Kentucky pastime of the Rupp era in particular. His inaugural squad was tagged "Pitino's Bombinos"; later came the "The Unforgettables" of 1991–92—the from-the-heart amalgamation of Richie Farmer, Deron Feldhaus, John Pelphrey, Sean Woods, et al.

In eight short seasons, Pitino had compiled a glitzy 219–50 mark, third best all time behind Rupp and Hall in UK annals. But more than that, he had administered salve to the wounded state of the Wildcat Nation—from Majestic to Monkeys Eyebrow—dazed by the shattering events of "Sutton Death." With Pitino's championship came a Renaissance of the faithful, the clouds parting once again. The Cats were back.

They had it before you, they had it during you, they'll have it when you're gone.

Al McGuire
on Kentucky's tradition

⚫ ⚫ ⚫

Kentucky is the Roman Empire of college basketball.

Robert Lindsey
Lexington, Kentucky

⚫ ⚫ ⚫

We feel that every boy who puts on a Kentucky uniform just plays a little better than he would in one of another color.

Adolph Rupp
head coach (1931–72)

⚫ ⚫ ⚫

There will be a Martian in the White House before there's a black coach on the bench where Adolph Rupp once sat.

Billy Reed
Louisville Courier-Journal, 1985

SMITHSONIAN

After program-changing turnabouts at both Tulsa and Georgia, where he led the Bulldogs to the 1996–97 SEC Tournament championship game (a loss, ironically, to Kentucky), Tubby Smith brought crafty rural know-how and big-program success to Lexington as Rick Pitino's successor in 1997. Smith, though, was no stranger to Wildcat Country, having served as an assistant on Pitino's 1990 and '91 staffs.

In a spectacular debut with the Blue and White, the fledgling UK mentor won the national championship—the first coach since Cincinnati's Ed Jucker in 1961 to win the NCAA title in his first year at a school. Through 2005, Smith has led the Cats to five regular-season SEC titles, five SEC Tournament crowns, and eight straight NCAA Tournament appearances.

The irony of African-American Smith's placement at the head of Kentucky basketball cannot be overlooked in light of the Wildcats' well-documented provincialism and foot-dragging reluctance to embrace integration in the 1960s. But from every angle, Smith is a perfect fit with UK.

THE
BIG BLUE

*K*entucky's unmatched eminence in collegiate basketball isn't just about Beard, Groza, Hagan, Nash, Issel, Grevey, Macy, Walker (Sky and Antoine), Mashburn, Mercer, and Prince. It's about Ken Rollins and Cliff Barker, the glue among the Fabulous Five; Tommy Kron and Larry Conley of Rupp's Runts; the Larry Steeles, Roger Hardens, and Richie Farmers.

Even before the golden years of Adolph Rupp began to churn toward greatness in the mid-1940s, Kentucky wrapped itself around a bevy of solid, reliable producers like Carey Spicer, Frenchy DeMoisey, LeRoy Edwards, and the great Aggie Sale—all from the late 1920s to mid-'30s.

Look deep into the soul of Kentucky Blue and you'll see the spirits of hundreds of dedicated and even over-achieving players that tint the special fabric that is UK basketball.

I wasn't successful in teaching that shot to any of the other boys. Frenchy was the only one able to make a go of it. It made him an All-American.

Adolph Rupp

*on developing the hook shot with center
John "Frenchy" DeMoisey, March 1931*

* * *

He had a lot better moves around the basket than most centers did at that time. He was much stronger in the upper body and had a good touch for the basket in close.

Paul McBrayer

*guard (1928–30)/assistant coach (1935–43),
on Helms Foundation Player of the Year
LeRoy Edwards (1935)*

* * *

He had a good close-in jump shot, an excellent hook shot with either hand, and could rebound above the basket.

David Lawrence

teammate of LeRoy Edwards in 1935

The 1934–35 season was the only one LeRoy Edwards played at UK, but because of him it was memorable. He was named All-SEC and All-American and the Helms Foundation Player of the Year— and he was only a sophomore. Unfortunately for the Wildcats and their faithful fans, his was a spirit more akin to that of the "do-your-own-thing" sixties than the Depression thirties.

Bert Nelli
Steve Nelli
authors

*   *   *

I can't do my best on the tea and toast Coach Rupp gives us before a game. Why, if they would give me a couple of beefsteaks before a game, I could really play. It takes a couple of beefsteaks to carry you up and down the floor.

LeRoy Edwards
center (1934–35)

He could bust the cable over the Golden Gate Bridge.

Adolph Rupp

*on the strength of 1935 All-America center
LeRoy Edwards. Rupp named Dan Issel,
Mike Pratt, and Pat Riley his next-strongest
players, in that order*

● ● ●

Cliff Barker was the old man of the group. He became 27 in January of that year of the Fabulous Five. He was shot down while serving as an engineer and gunner aboard a B-17 bomber and was taken prisoner. It was while fooling around with a volleyball during his long period of confinement that he developed the ball-handling skill that was to earn him the reputation of a true "Houdini of the Hoops," "Basketball Banshee," and "Super Magician."

Russell Rice

author/former UK assisant athlethic director

Six-one forward Cliff Barker . . . often used behind-the-back passes and in time developed a bounce pass with so much spin it would come to the receiver at a 45-degree angle.

Dave Kindred

❂ ❂ ❂

That was the year [1948] we were best. And Kenny Rollins was the reason. He was the catalyst, the unselfish one.

Ralph Beard

❂ ❂ ❂

The six-foot one-inch, 160-pound sophomore, with a reputation for being "right smart" on both defense and offense, is expected to see action at guard. . . . Although weak eyes make it necessary for him to wear his glasses taped to his temples during the game, Hall is not noticeably bothered by the "extra eyes."

UK 1949 Media Guide
on Joe B. Hall

Without Wah Wah Jones, it's safe to say UK never could have gone on to a 28–2 record that season [1946] or to UK's first national tournament championship—the National Invitation Tournament title. He was a great player for four years, becoming one of the celebrated Fabulous Five as a junior and going to the Olympics that same year [1948], playing on two NCAA championship teams, and making All-America as a senior. With all that, though, he had to take third billing his last three years at UK. "Groza, Beard, and Jones," the phrase went, or "Beard, Groza, and Jones."

Tev Laudeman

author

AP/WIDE WORLD PHOTOS

Wallace "Wah Wah" Jones

R upp once told Larry Pursiful that every time the player shot the basketball, he thought it was going in.

Jamie H. Vaught
author,
on the great outside-shooting guard
from 1960 through '62

❊ ❊ ❊

I don't think I realized how much Tom Kron and Larry Conley sacrificed to allow Louie and me to be the shooters on the team, to become All-Americans. They were the real leaders—the spirit and the glue. Louie and I were just the finish.

Pat Riley
forward (1965–67)/SEC Player of the Year (1966)/
All-NCAA Final Four team (1966)/
All-SEC (1966)

❊ ❊ ❊

B ob Tallent, Jim LeMaster, Tommy Porter, Cliff Berger, Steve Clevenger, Brad Bounds, Larry Lentz, Gary Gamble, Gene Stewart, Bob Windsor. They sweated as much as we did. They just happened to sweat a little less on game days.

Tommy Kron
on Rupp's Runts, 1965–66

Jimmy Dan Conner was "Mr. Basketball" in Kentucky as a high school player. He was a very tough competitor, the guy you'd like to have as a foxhole buddy. He was the leader on the team as a senior and really was at his best in the big games. He was a tough defensive player who could dominate an opponent.

Cawood Ledford
legendary voice of the Wildcats

Jimmy Dan was our emotional leader. When we started to sag, he would do something spectacular to bring us back up. He would pop us in the chest and say, "Come on, we gotta win. Let's play."

Kevin Grevey
forward (1973–75),
on Conner

A 6–5 power-dunking forward with a bruising presence inside yet athletic enough to be a valuable weapon in the open court, James Lee was a key role player on the 1978 NCAA championship team.

Michael Bradley
author

* * *

Dirk Minniefield was an old-school point guard who lived to set up his team-mates. The 6–3 Lexington product was so good in the early 1980s that he remains Kentucky's all-time leader in assists [646]. Minniefield also led the Cats in steals three consecutive years.

Michael Bradley

* * *

Bennett seems to be a catalyst for this team. I don't know if I've ever had a freshman who had that much leadership influence on a team.

Joe B. Hall
on 1984 freshman Winston Bennett

If you've got two 7-footers against one 7-footer, the intimidation should work out about two-to-one. That's about the way it worked.

Guy Lewis

University of Houston head coach,
on UK's Melvin Turpin and Sam Bowie vs.
Houston's Akeem Olajuwon, January 22, 1984

FAST BREAK: *The Wildcats beat the Cougars, 74–67.*

● ● ●

He's the quarterback of our squad. When you see me get a blocked shot, that's probably because Roger Harden told me to get in position.

Sam Bowie

on the Wildcat point guard of 1983–86

N ow, I wish I could go back and play with the confidence I have in myself as a person. As a player, I would probably be 10 times better now than I was back at that time.

Dwane Casey

guard (1976–79)/assistant coach (1987–89)

● ● ●

E d Davender's name doesn't roll off the tongues of Kentucky fans when they discuss UK's foremost players, but there is no denying the guard's significant contributions. He's the only player in school history to score more than 1,500 points and record over 400 assists.

Michael Bradley

● ● ●

D eron Feldhaus, a key player on Rick Pitino's Unforgettables and a member of Kentucky's 1,000-point club, gave the Wildcats a rare blend of interior toughness and perimeter shooting accuracy.

Michael Bradley

A smooth distributor who displayed a sweet outside stroke and a deadly eye from the foul line, Travis Ford set a UK season record with 101 three-point field goals in 1993 and wound up as the Wildcats' No. 2 career free throw shooter.

Michael Bradley

● ● ●

D erek Anderson is the premier two-guard in the country. What we see every day from him in practice is incredible.

Rick Pitino

● ● ●

A ll I can say is thank you, Ohio State, for giving us Derek Anderson.

Rick Pitino

FAST BREAK: Anderson transferred to Kentucky after his sophomore year at Ohio State.

Where'd he come from?

David Hobbs

*former Alabama head coach/current Kentucky
associate head coach,
on UK reserve Michael Bradley, who scored 10
points and grabbed six rebounds in 14 minutes
of play in Kentucky's 82–71 SEC Tournament
win over his Crimson Tide in 1998*

● ● ●

I think he is one of the most underrated guards in the country. He did a great job of penetrating and pitching. He's the guy who makes their team go.

Steve Wojciechowski

*Duke player,
on Wildcat guard Wayne Turner,
1998 South Region MVP*

● ● ●

The 6–10 center from Canada is Kentucky's career blocked-shots leader with 268 rejections and was named UK's best defender in his last three seasons.

Michael Bradley

on Jamaal Magloire (1997–2000)

P owerful and relentless, Keith Bogans, a strong driver and capable finisher near the basket, made an immediate mark with his ability to score and willingness to play physical defense.

Michael Bradley

* * *

J eff Sheppard came here as a highly-recruited player and had to sit behind Tony Delk for three years. Also he had to sit behind Ron Mercer and Derek Anderson for a year. And then he redshirted because they were back again. He became the MVP in the Final Four. That's a remarkable feat.

Tubby Smith

* * *

J ust a freshman? Ask anyone who has faced his ballhawking D if his inexperience shows.

ESPN the Magazine
on Rajon Rondo,
ranked No. 4 nationally among 2004–05
defensive-minded "Guard Dogs"

R ajon Rondo might be the most fearless freshman in the land.

Pat Forde

● ● ●

R ondo being Rondo is a major element of Kentucky being a national contender. He creates havoc on defense with his long arms and ability to hawk the ball. He creates havoc on offense with his ability to get into the lane on anybody. He's unafraid to stick his nose into the lane and snatch rebounds. His absolute assuredness running one of the most high-profile shows in Hoopsworld separates him from other teenage point guards. And more than a few older point guards as well.

Pat Forde

WILDCAT CHARACTER

C oach Hall was a very tough coach, a very disciplined coach. He taught me not only about basketball but also how to handle myself off the floor. Through his discipline, I became a better player and person. In a work situation, one has to be disciplined to do certain things on the job and do things right and that's really what he was trying to do. Maybe not all his working was just for the basketball sense, but in preparing an individual for the real world when one is finished with basketball.

Kyle Macy
point guard (1978–80)/All-America (1979, '80)

He convinced us we could do things we didn't know we could do.

Frank Ramsey
*Kentucky guard (1951, '52, '54),
on Adolph Rupp*

* * *

I've never known a successful person in any walk of life who hasn't been disciplined. Discipline is necessary, whether you are a basketball player or a businessman. I am referring to an internal discipline—discipline of time, discipline of behavior.

Eddie Sutton

* * *

I want the players to live like the rest of the student body. Once you leave here, you have to be able to deal with people and you can't prepare for that living off by yourself.

Rick Pitino

E veryone has a desire to do well, but you have to have dedication. You have to pay the price to do well. You can't just wish you were good, you have to work at it and be dedicated to the task.

Eddie Sutton

I can't tell you over the years the number of things that UK coaches from Fran Curci to Joe B. Hall to Eddie Sutton to Rick Pitino have done, such as writing out a letter to a little kid who has a terminal illness. Those people would rather have a Kentucky Wildcat or Kentucky coach autograph something for them than have a good day.

Oscar Combs
CatsPause.com

We have a rule. You don't speak unless you can improve the silence.

Adolph Rupp

* * *

I told the players they will need a substitute for the goal of making the NCAA Tournament. They will have fun. And I told them to think about their careers and lives. That's more important than the NCAA Tournament.

Rick Pitino

while the Wildcats were on probation in the early 1990s

* * *

Loyalty without principle is fanaticism.

Bret Bearup

We said, "You guys need to make up for the loss of Chuck." They'd never seen Chuck hurt before. I'll be honest, I don't think I'd ever seen Chuck hurt. It showed me what our kids are all about.

Orlando "Tubby" Smith

head coach (1998–),
on the fortitude of his 2005 Wildcats, who lost
the services of star senior forward Chuck
Hayes—who had never missed a game or a
practice in his four years due to injury—
with a broken nose against Tennessee.
UK went on to beat the Vols, 84–62

● ● ●

To Louie Dampier, "Pulling a Riley" means to think about things—especially basketball or life—at great length.

C. Ray Hall

Louisville Courier-Journal,
March 30, 1986

There are a lot of advantages in being disorganized. That way every day is a surprise. Besides, if you're organized, you have to organize everybody else.

Tommy Kron
guard (1964–66)

❋ ❋ ❋

I think that one thing you can't do in life is look ahead and want for something else. If you want for something else, you are tired of what you are doing.

Rick Pitino

❋ ❋ ❋

You figure if you give everything you have, you get what you want. But sometimes, you don't.

Chuck Hayes
*after the Cats' double-OT loss to Michigan State
in the 2005 NCAA Austin Regional final*

T o me, basketball was everything.

Ralph Beard
guard (1946–49)

❂ ❂ ❂

H ow badly did Joe B. Hall want to play for the Wildcats? You be the judge. As a freshman Hall underwent a tonsillectomy on a Friday. By Wednesday he was back at practice. By the end of the same week he was returned to the hospital because of the bleeding.

Rick Bozich
writer,
Louisville Courier-Journal,
on Joe B. Hall, the Wildcat player (1949)
and future UK assistant and head coach

Big dreams start with little dreams.

Tubby Smith

◉ ◉ ◉

Sometimes things can come too easy for you. We . . . got complacent. We struggled, but we really persevered.

Tubby Smith
on his Cats' 82–71 SEC Tournament opening-game win over Alabama in 1998

◉ ◉ ◉

You have to have longevity. Patience.

Tubby Smith

◉ ◉ ◉

We're the big bully, and the big bully doesn't back down.

Ravi Moss
guard (2003–06)

HEROES AND ICONS

R alph Beard is what this game is all about.

Clair Bee
legendary basketball coach

● ● ●

H e's the greatest basketball player I ever saw.

Adolph Rupp
on all-time Kentucky guard Ralph Beard

Aggie would shoot off balance, falling down, or sitting on the floor if he had to.

George Yates

Wildcat player (1930, '31, '33),
on 1931, '33 UK teammate Aggie Sale

⚾ ⚾ ⚾

This gangling youngster was to go high—to the very zenith before he finished at UK. He would twice be voted All-America, would captain the Wildcats as a senior, be voted Player of the Year for the entire nation, and would lead UK to its first national championship.

Tev Laudeman

on Aggie Sale

FAST BREAK: *Kentucky was named Helms National Champion in 1933 and 1954.*

⚾ ⚾ ⚾

Oh, I'm too busy scoring to worry about defense.

Aggie Sale

center (1931–33)

Years later, Adolph was to tell me several times that Aggie Sale might have
been the best player he ever coached.

Harry Lancaster
*UK assistant coach under Adolph Rupp
(1943–44, 1947–69)/volunteer assistant
under Joe B. Hall (1981)*

● ● ●

If Kentucky ever had a player in whom
the fires of competitive zeal burned with
a greater roar than in Ralph Beard, his
name is a secret.

Dave Kindred

His first basket was his potty chair. He'd throw a little rubber ball at the chair. As he got older, he used the cutaway part of his high chair. Then we put a miniature basket over his bed. Then we tacked it up on the kitchen door. Finally we had to move it outside in the yard.

Sue Beard

Ralph Beard's mother

● ● ●

Beard scored on that lightning layup with either hand, shot well from outside, and played defense as if points scored on him were personal insults.

Dave Kindred

● ● ●

Beard is absolutely the best I ever saw.

Bud Browning

coach,
whose AAU champion Phillips 66ers defeated
Kentucky in the finals of the 1948 Olympic Trials

Ralph Beard

A nation of newspaper readers often comes to know its sports heroes by the repeated use of photographs capturing the man at his moment: Babe Ruth swinging a 40-ounce bat, looking skyward; Arnold Palmer with that mile-wide smile in celebration of a successful putt. For Kentuckians who adored Ralph Beard, he forever will be the little guy, stern-visaged and hard-muscled, flying . . . always flying . . . for another layup at the end of a sudden sprint that left the enemy wondering where he went.

Dave Kindred

● ● ●

I'd rather be a real athlete, like Ralph.

Frank Beard
former PGA golf star and step-brother of Ralph Beard

Extremely quick off the dribble and relentless on the defensive end, Beard often overwhelmed opponents. He sparked the Wildcats' pressure tactics at both ends of the floor, forcing turnovers and turning them into easy buckets.

Michael Bradley

● ● ●

Groza's excellence as a basketball player was due to his remarkable speed for a man of his size and an uncanny ability to control both the offensive and defensive backboards. Rupp termed him one of the best rebounders the game had ever known.

Russell Rice

● ● ●

He was a big, hulking bear of a man who moved with deceptive grace.

The Associated Press

describing 6–7 three-time All-America center
Alex Groza

Alex Groza

He accomplished with force the little he couldn't do with his astonishing quickness. As a pro center, he was second only to George Mikan, who was later voted the Outstanding Player of the Half-Century.

Dave Kindred
on Alex Groza

In 1949 Alex Groza became the third UK star to be named the Helms Foundation Basketball Player of the Year. Two years later another Wildcat center, Bill Spivey, became Player of the Year.

Bert Nelli
Steve Nelli

Alex Groza, though only an 18-year-old freshman, already displayed the perfect basketball hands, the great team spirit, and the uncanny ability at hitting the basket that would later mark his play as a member of the Fabulous Five. Although the 6–7 pivotman played only in UK's first eleven games of the campaign, he scored enough points to lead the team in scoring for the entire 1945 season.

Bert Nelli
Steve Nelli

You don't replace a Caruso with a barbershop singer.

Adolph Rupp
on filling Alex Groza's shoes after the young
center reported to the army, January 15, 1945

R ed Auerbach called him the best sixth man in history because Ramsey made things happen when he entered a game. More versatile than Hagan, Ramsey could play either out front or inside. He invented ways to get the ball in the bucket. Under pressure, he was majestic.

Dave Kindred

on Frank Ramsey (1951–52, '54)

❁ ❁ ❁

I f we win by 30, Frank might only get you three, but if we win by three, Frank will get you 30.

Adolph Rupp

on 1952, '54 All-America guard Frank Ramsey

❁ ❁ ❁

T he picture Frank Ramsey evoked was this: if UK absolutely had to have a basket, he would run over someone and get it.

Tev Laudeman

Cliff Hagan

C liff Hagan drove in for a layup, missed it, then tipped it in from the other side. I had never seen anything like that.

Phil Grawemeyer
forward (1954–56)

● ● ●

T hough only 6–4, he was a dominant frontcourt player capable of burning opponents with his hook shot or humbling them on the backboards.

Michael Bradley
on forward Cliff Hagan (1951, '52, '54)

● ● ●

H agan was a work of art in the pivot—all grace and all strength, an extraordinary jumper. He scored on every kind of shot, but witnesses remember best the hook shot put up so smoothly the ball seemed to float.

Dave Kindred
on Cliff Hagan

I was going to break him of that hook shot, but every time I got ready to make him stop using the thing, he would hit four or five in a row, and I'd say to myself, "I'll break him next week."

Adolph Rupp
on Cliff Hagan

If I had to put a man on the free throw line and my life depended on whether he made it or not, Vernon Hatton is the man I'd want to shoot it.

Harry Lancaster

He's the best I've played against. I put him in a class with Art Heyman and Jeff Mullins of Duke. I didn't realize Nash was so big and strong.

Yogi Poteet
North Carolina player,
on Cotton Nash, December 17, 1962

● ● ●

Cotton Nash was so talented and he moved on the floor with such fluid ease that the coaches thought he was loafing. They thought he wasn't trying. He moved so easily that they thought he wasn't hustling.

Larry Pursiful
guard (1960–62)

O ne of the most charismatic and popular Wildcats of all time. Also one of the true greats. There seemed to be no limit to what he could do on a basketball court. He was smooth and graceful, sheer poetry in motion. Had a deadly outside jumper and enough slithery one-on-one moves to get to the rack against the finest defenders. Literally carried the program on his back during his three years at UK. He earned All-America and All-SEC honors in each of his three seasons. Left as the school's all-time leading scorer with 1,770 points in only 78 games.

Tom Wallace
author,
on Cotton Nash

I never knew what a basketball was until I moved to Indiana. I was a teenager by then and in New Jersey [where he formerly lived] there was only one sport that you played and that was baseball. We didn't know that there was such a game as that big ball you bounce with.

Cotton Nash
center/forward (1962–64)/three-time
All-America (1962, '63, '64)

● ● ●

He wears contact lenses on the court, horned rims off the court, and might be accused of being Clark Kent, except that he could never fit into a phone booth to change clothes.

Frank Deford
on Pat Riley,
Sports Illustrated, *March 7, 1966*

JUMPIN' PAT FLASH

Long before he made a name in the NBA as the championship coach of the Los Angeles Lakers and Miami Heat, Pat Riley was a Wildcat, and a jumping phenom at that.

At just 6–3, Riley, considered the Cats' best all-around player, handled center-jump chores as a famous forward for Rupp's Runts—the game, pit-bull-tenacious scrappers of the mid-'60s that were ranked No. 1 right up until the NCAA championship game loss against Texas Western in 1966.

Incredibly, Riley at one point won 46 of 51 center jumps that season, usually against opponents five to six inches taller.

But the crafty Riley let on that there was a little more to it than that. "Harry Lancaster [former UK assistant coach] taught me a little trick," Riley once explained. "As I went up, I would plant my elbow on the other guy's shoulder, and he'd lift me up."

H e could withstand intimidation.

Joe B. Hall
on Pat Riley

* * *

G od taught Louie [Dampier] how to shoot, and I took credit for it.

Adolph Rupp

* * *

T he best outside shooter I ever saw.

Adolph Rupp
on Louie Dampier

He has the natural ability to want the last shot, the tremendous confidence in his shooting to win the pressure game. . . . If he played on a team with Jerry West or Nate Archibald or Walt Frazier—those guys who take two people to guard them— Louie Dampier would be a household name across the country. He would be a consistent 20-plus scorer and probably would be referred to as one for the greatest jump shooters from 17 to 25 feet ever to play the game.

Hubie Brown

basketball analyst and former coach

● ● ●

Louie Dampier can play basketball anywhere. He could be an outstanding asset to any league, any team, any place. . . . He's a pro's pro, and that's the highest compliment I can give him.

Hubie Brown

AP/WIDE WORLD PHOTOS

Louie Dampier

He is Kentucky's all-time leading scorer, a big man who could score inside or on 18-foot jumpers. Harry Lancaster, for 20 years Rupp's right-hand man, said Issel was UK's best player ever.

Dave Kindred
on Dan Issel

❋ ❋ ❋

Dan Issel is one of the greatest Kentucky players I never saw play. I wish I could have.

John M. Quimby
author

Dan Issel pressures LSU's Pete Maravich to make a no-look pass.

After playing 15 years of professional basketball, my four favorite years of basketball are the four years that I spent at UK.

Dan Issel
center (1968–70),
UK's all-time leading scorer and rebounder

❋ ❋ ❋

The thing I remember most about Dan Issel was the great work ethic and the outstanding improvement that he made from his freshman year to his sophomore year. . . . I've never seen a player make as dramatic improvement as Dan Issel made.

Joe B. Hall

❋ ❋ ❋

By the time he left UK, Issel had established 23 school and SEC records during his varsity career at Kentucky.

Jamie H. Vaught

J ack "Goose" Givens was a ballet dancer in sneakers.

Cawood Ledford

* * *

G ivens had a great night. He gave us a fine effort, helped us inside with his rebounding and kept hitting that little dishrag jump shot of his. He's done it so many times that you kind of take it for granted. He's done it 10 or 12 times this year.

Joe B. Hall
*on Jack Givens's performance in the Cats' 1975
Final Four semifinal win over Syracuse*

O ne of the finest big men in a program filled with them, the strong yet mobile Robey teamed with Mike Phillips and James Lee to form an imposing front wall in the late 1970s. Robey contributed mightily to Kentucky's 1978 national champions, averaging 14.4 points and a team-high 8.2 rebounds.

Michael Bradley
on center Rick Robey (1975–78)

* * *

H e gives us a touch of finesse and sometimes a touch of brains. He comes through in the clutch. He's a coach on the floor.

Joe B. Hall
on Kyle Macy, 1978

* * *

H e's the greatest guard in the nation.

Bobby Knight
Indiana University head coach,
on Kyle Macy

Kyle will make us an intelligent, smart, finesse-type ball club. We have not had a finesse guard in quite a while and we have not had a guard with the leadership qualities of Macy. The closest was Jimmy Dan Conner. Kyle is an excellent outside shooter, passer, penetrator. He's a quarterback on the floor.

Joe B. Hall

● ● ●

If any player ever came to Kentucky with the fanfare that preceded Rex Chapman, it's lost to history.

Cawood Ledford

FAST BREAK: Chapman, a two-time high school All-American at Apollo High in Owensboro, Kentucky, was named the state's AP Male Athlete of the Year and selected as its prestigious "Mr. Basketball."

E d Davender nicknamed Rex Chapman "Rosey." As in "Roosevelt" Chapman. As in, "Here's one of the brethren coming off the brickyards of the inner city who can flick the switch on a spin-dribble 18-footer as smoothly as he can turn up the volume on a ghetto-blaster.

Jim Terhune
Louisville Courier-Journal, *December 27, 1986*

● ● ●

I believe anything he shoots. Even though he's only a freshman, he's got to be one of the top guards in the country.

Herbert Crook
University of Louisville,
on UK freshman phenom Rex Chapman, 1986

Chapman was somewhat overwhelmed by his great "White Hope" popularity at Kentucky. He was under heavy microscopic watch from Kentucky fans and the news media. He was "King Rex." Even Lexington was sometimes referred to as "Rexington" in coffee shop conversations.

Jamie H. Vaught

❀ ❀ ❀

He reminds me of Jerry West. I hesitate to say that because Jerry West was probably one of the top 15 players of all time.

Eddie Sutton

on Rex Chapman

❀ ❀ ❀

A two-time All-American and Kentucky's second-leading all-time scorer, Kenny Walker was one of UK's toughest, most exciting players. Nicknamed "Sky" for his great leaping ability, he was twice named SEC Player of the Year.

Tom Wallace

on the Wildcat forward from 1983 through '86

His hands are awesome, and his lower body's so strong. From coaching Charles Oakley and Bernard King and watching Karl Malone and Kevin McHale, I know about NBA moves, and Jamal has all of theirs.

Rick Pitino
on Jamal Mashburn

● ● ●

Mashburn is an imported update of Wildcat great Dan Issel; quiet, relentless, a scoring threat both inside and out, and a stoic who gets his teammates going on the fast break with his work on the boards.

Alexander Wolff
Sports Illustrated, *November 23, 1992*

He has the body of a blacksmith and the touch of a surgeon.

Tom Konchalski
HSBI Report,
on Jamal Mashburn

* * *

Mashburn was a rare combination of outside firepower and interior muscle. Nicknamed "Monster Mash" for his ability to dominate opponents close to the basket, he brought mega-star skills to a starting unit featuring plucky seniors known as the Unforgettables.

Michael Bradley

* * *

It was like giving an atomic bomb to a terrorist.

Bob Oliva
coach, New York's Christ the King High School,
on Jamal Mashburn playing for Rick Pitino

That's like asking Pat Riley, "Were you concerned about Magic and Worthy and those guys putting on a show?" That's what this is. It's entertainment.

Rick Pitino

when asked if he was concerned about Wildcats Derek Anderson and Ron Mercer—"the Air Pair"—turning a fast break into a show

* * *

Out of all of the players I've ever coached, watching him grow as a young man is the most special moment of my life in coaching basketball.

Rick Pitino

on forward Antoine Walker (1995–96)

A 6–8 forward with good shooting range, Antoine Walker could feed the post and set up teammates on the break—skills that made him a perfect fit for Rick Pitino's system.

Michael Bradley

* * *

R on Mercer easily ranks among the most supremely gifted and multi-dimensional Wildcats of all-time. Although known more for his slashing drives and arena-rattling dunks, he was also capable of burning defenses with his perimeter jumper. Was consensus first-team All-America, SEC Player of the Year [1997], and MVP of the NCAA West Regional [1997].

Tom Wallace

A spindly 6–9 forward with a sweet shooting touch, Tayshaun Prince led the Cats in scoring as a sophomore [13.3 average] and a senior [17.5]. He was at his best in his next-to-last UK game, erupting for 41 points against Tulsa in the 2002 NCAA Tournament.

Michael Bradley

LEGENDARY
COACHES

By crimminy, my coaching is worth a technical foul anytime.

Adolph Rupp

● ● ●

Rupp. Like "love" and "hate," it's a four-letter word.

C. Ray Hall

A governor cannot succeed himself in the Commonwealth of Kentucky, and a horse can run only once in the Derby, but as long as Adolph Rupp is around, the Bluegrass will never suffer from a lack of continuity. For 36 years, in a land of colonels, he has been the only Baron, a man of consummate pride and well-earned privilege . . . at age 64, he continues to pursue the only challenge left—trying to top himself. And that is some tough act to follow.

Frank Deford
Sports Illustrated,
March 7, 1966

● ● ●

He was not only an iconic presence, but an ironic one: He could be in the action, and above it.

C. Ray Hall
on Adolph Rupp

C oach Rupp knew how to sharpen iron with iron.

Jim Dinwiddie
UK player (1969–71)

◈ ◈ ◈

H e set records for vanity that will never be broken.

Dave Kindred
on Adolph Rupp

◈ ◈ ◈

H e was never totally, totally satisfied.

Ralph Beard
on Rupp

◈ ◈ ◈

H e had the ability to look into the future and decide what to do. He made a decision, started at the beginning, and worked toward his goals.

Ed Beck
UK player (1956–58),
on Adolph Rupp

Rupp once said you could judge a player's aggressiveness by the way he attacked his steak; he watched Cliff Hagan devour a steak and figure he'd do the same to opponents. Hagan ended up owning a chain of steak houses.

C. Ray Hall

● ● ●

I always got the feeling he liked the country boys—kids from the mountains. I think he had a special feeling for them.

G. J. Smith
Wildcat player (1973–75),
on Adolph Rupp

● ● ●

Rupp, who has never been encumbered by modesty, used to teach a basketball course at UK, and he would always give all of his students "As." Rupp's reasoning was simply that no one could learn basketball from Adolph Rupp and not get an A.

Frank Deford

AP/WIDE WORLD PHOTOS

Adolph Rupp

oach Rupp could be mean but not mean-spirited. It's just that he was very disciplined. Most coaches kick you in the butt one minute and pat you on the back the next. Rupp just kicked you in the butt all the time.

Dan Issel

* * *

he first thing I noticed about meeting coach Rupp was his handshake. It was real soft. I thought, after hearing some of the stories about Coach Rupp and how hard he was on people, he'd have a real, real tough grip. When he had the soft handshake, my immediate reaction was, "Well, he doesn't seem to be that tough."

Louie Dampier
guard (1965–67)

I grew up listening to Dr. Allen's team [at Kansas] and Mr. [Adolph] Rupp's teams [at Kentucky]. I used to pretend I was out there, playing for Coach Allen and Mr. Rupp, and being somebody.

Eddie Sutton

❀ ❀ ❀

Rupp's teams from the beginning were models of simplicity and fire. They took hold of the ball and ran.

Dave Kindred

❀ ❀ ❀

Sarcasm was only one of Rupp's weapons. The others included showmanship, superstition, Scripture [occasionally], stubbornness, and a supreme self-confidence.

C. Ray Hall

I will lift up mine eyes unto the hills, whence cometh my help.

Psalm 121:1

Adolph Rupp's favorite Biblical passage and his guiding principle in recruiting

● ● ●

He was involved in many, many things. He wasn't a one-dimensional person. He was a three-, four-, or five-dimensional person.

Herky Rupp

the Baron's son and a 1961 UK basketball letterman, on his father

● ● ●

There wasn't a whole lot of difference between them. They were both demanding that you do it the right way and give all you've got 100 percent. I always did that so I got along real well with both of them.

Wallace "Wah Wah" Jones

forward (1946–49), on playing football at UK under Bear Bryant and basketball for Adolph Rupp

He was a man of many dimensions, not just the basketball coach. He was more than that, having a lot of other interests. One of the smartest individuals who ever lived in the state of Kentucky, he read books and kept *U.S. News and World Report, Wall Street Journal, Forbes,* and the *American Hereford Journal.* He was well educated, obtaining his master's degree in educational administration from Columbia University in New York in 1930 before coming to Kentucky. A successful farmer himself, he was elected president of a well-known state cattle organization many times.

Jamie H. Vaught
on Adolph Rupp

I don't think he gave the same image publicly as he did privately. Coach Rupp was a big man. He was about 6–4 and he was a pretty towering figure when you were up next to him, unless you were somebody like Dan Issel or Alex Groza. But he had this commanding presence about him. I suppose the last 15 years of his life I was as close to him as anybody around. He was very warm, understanding, very bright, articulate, very well read. He was a very well-educated man. He had a great sense of knowledge of history, and we had more intellectual discussions than anything. . . . We always had something to talk about.

Claude Vaughan
former UK trainer/tutor/longtime friend
of Rupp

He thought that when a Kentucky baby was born, the mother had two wishes for him: to grow up to be like another native son, Abraham Lincoln, and to play basketball for Adolph Rupp.

Russell Rice

on Rupp

● ● ●

I think one of his great attributes was that he didn't take things personally. I think that's one of the reasons he got along well with the press. He was great copy but he didn't let things get to him. I think that's one reason he coached as long as he did because he could stand the pressure better than anyone I've ever encountered.

Claude Vaughan

on Adolph Rupp

C oach Rupp was a very easy coach to play for . . . I wasn't intimidated by him, even though we respected him a great deal. Before I went to UK, I heard lots of tales about how mean he was, but it didn't turn out to be that way. I enjoyed playing for coach Rupp. He was a comedian so he kept us laughing all the time. We really enjoyed being around him.

Terry Mills
guard (1969–71)

● ● ●

I t takes six or eight years to get over play- ing for coach Rupp. Once you get over it, you get to like him.

Vernon Hatton
guard (1956–58)/All-America (1958)

He was very tough to play for . . . if a player came in and wanted to play basketball and was serious about it and getting his education, there weren't any problems.

Louie Dampier

He was more of an actor, I think, than anything else. I understood that more when I came back as an assistant coach. I realized that he was acting the entire time. He would have been a champion in Hollywood.

Dickie Parsons
Wildcat player (1959–61)/
assistant coach (1970–80),
on Adolph Rupp

I was intimidated by coach Rupp. He was very distant. You never saw him except on the floor. Occasionally, you might run into him in outer offices or somewhere on campus but rarely would he bother to even speak to you. You showed up for practice and did what was expected of you. That was all the contact you had with coach Rupp.

Joe B. Hall

● ● ●

With us, there was no joking, no laughing, no whistling, no singing, no nothing. Just basketball. When we traveled, for instance, he [Rupp] often communicated with us through the team manager.

Alex Groza
*center (1945, 1947–49)/three-time All-America
(1947–49)/two-time NCAA Final Four MVP
(1948, '49)/1948 Olympic basketball
gold medalist*

Coach Rupp and the 1949 national champion Kentucky Wildcats

Everyone who played for coach Rupp was intimidated by him. Even the servicemen that came back, mature men who had been through prison camps, war, and everything else were intimidated by Coach Rupp, and those who weren't completely intimidated by Rupp were intimidated by Harry Lancaster. The 1–2 punch just about got everyone.

Joe B. Hall
a Rupp assistant (1966–72) and later head coach at Kentucky

Adolph Frederick Rupp was round of face and body, but lean and angular of thought, and brutally direct of expression. He was sharp of tongue, short of temper, long of memory, and large of ego. He had little use for fools, jesters, moral lapsers, or freethinkers.

C. Ray Hall

All you ever heard was the bounce of the ball. Coach Rupp called it his classroom. He wanted total concentration.

Dickie Parsons

* * *

He was the most brilliant basketball coach of this or any other time. Or he was the lucky beneficiary of Southern hospitality, scoring most of his victories against schools that took basketball about as seriously as badminton. [He once beat Georgia by 77. His players grabbed a surreal 108 rebounds against Ole Miss, a team that went 0–36, against Rupp.] One coaching rival, Johnny Dee, likened Rupp's rule of the South to hauling a hockey team to Texas and taking on all comers.

C. Ray Hall

I think Adolph slipped a bit as a coach right after we had the Runts. We lost all those close games and he'd sit there on the bench late in the game and almost panic. He had lost his grip as a great coach. The players were aware of it.

Harry Lancaster

❀ ❀ ❀

Despite his many records and achievements, Rupp was in some ways a tragic figure during the last part of his career. These years were filled with physical pain and an increasing sense of professional frustration, in large part because of the spectacular success of John Wooden and the UCLA Bruins.

Bert Nelli
Steve Nelli

He was a very kind-hearted and good father. His image and demeanor on the floor were entirely different than they were at home. When he left the coliseum, he left basketball there.

Herky Rupp

● ● ●

My father was an entirely different person than most of these articles have painted him to be.

Herky Rupp

I 've done what I like to do. I've done it where I wanted to do it, with the people I wanted to do it with.

Joe B. Hall

● ● ●

C oach Hall was a very tough coach. He was a guy who set a lot of rules, regulations, and curfews, but I had a wonderful relationship with Coach Hall. He was a disciplinarian. He believed that hard work paid big dividends and he never was the type of guy who thought shortcuts were any way to success. I have nothing but respect for him.

Sam Bowie

He was trying to do some funny acts to get us loose. He took his tie off, messed his hair up, put one leg down in the big barrel trash can and unbuttoned his shirt. He was funny, but at that time we were so scared he couldn't have done anything to make us relax.

Dwane Casey

on Hall's attempt to calm his Cats before the 1978 NCAA finals against Duke

Coach Hall was misunderstood. He was very demanding on the players, but he had to be. Yet, off the floor he was compassionate. He cared a great deal about the players; he cared about the people in his program. He was very approachable as a head coach.

Joe Dean Jr.

assistant coach under Hall (1978–83)

J oe B. Hall not only followed The Man, he followed The Man who watched every move he made. This was a task as formidable as the task of following Wooden, Lombardi, or Bryant.

Rick Bozich

● ● ●

H e stood at center court at Assembly Hall in Bloomington and told Indiana coach Bob Knight that he would not back down even as the Hoosiers were pounding Kentucky by 24 points. Three months later, in Dayton, in the championship game of the NCAA Mideast Regional, Kentucky upset unbeaten and top-ranked Indiana for the right to advance to the NCAA Final Four. This was no longer Adolph Rupp's basketball program. This program belonged to Joe B. Hall.

Rick Bozich

ny student of sports knows that Joe B. Hall should be admired for the way he showed how to live with expectations of greatness while following a legend.

Rick Bozich

* * *

ne of the nation's winningest coaches in NCAA Division I, posting a 20-year career record of 430–164, Eddie Sutton finished his four-year stint at Kentucky with an 88–39 mark. But his coaching reputation had been tarnished. Things would never be the same. . . . He had become a fallen hero.

Jamie H. Vaught

* * *

e could coach a soft breeze into a hurricane.

Peter Vecsey
USA TODAY,
on Rick Pitino

My last three years as the UK broadcaster, Pitino was the coach. I got to know him quite well over that time and I must admit, they were the most enjoyable three years of my 39 with the Wildcats. To see him take a down-and-out program and immediately guide it to over-achieving was just great fun to be associated with. I still think his accomplishments border on a miracle.

Cawood Ledford

❋ ❋ ❋

To some UK fans, Rupp-Pitino is Old Testament God vs. New Testament God—wrath vs. redemption.

C. Ray Hall

❋ ❋ ❋

He's a basketball junkie. Just the hardest working guy I've ever been around and it carried over to this teams.

C. M. Newton
guard (1951)/athletic director (1989–2000),
on Pitino

We couldn't have hired anybody better than Rick Pitino. People talked about Pat Riley, this and that. Pat Riley wouldn't have come in and had the impact that Pitino has. John Thompson [Georgetown] and Dean Smith [North Carolina] wouldn't have. Nobody would have. It's Rick Pitino. It's him. His style of basketball is fun. It's entertaining. It's fun to talk about. It's fun to watch. He brought magic back to where it should be.

Bret Bearup

* * *

Rick Pitino is the man right now. At one time John Wooden was the man, and Dean Smith and Bobby Knight and Mike Krzyzewski. Well, right now Rick is the man. He's changed college basketball.

Bobby Cremins
former head coach, Georgia Tech

R upp, Hall, Sutton, and Pitino were four very different personalities. But they all had one thing in common . . . they were driven to win and each of them could flat coach basketball.

Cawood Ledford

* * *

W e lost the best coach in college basketball. Then we gained the best coach in college basketball.

Cameron Mills
*guard (1995–98),
on Tubby Smith replacing Rick Pitino
as head coach*

* * *

T ubby Smith has successfully demystified the position of UK head coach. There was always an imposing atmosphere around Rick Pitino that I think he wanted to exist to keep distractions to a minimum. It's something Dean Smith used to his advantage [at North Carolina] and that [former Indiana coach] Bob Knight perfected.

Mike DeCourcy
sportswriter/columnist

Pitino was a hard-driving taskmaster and Tubby Smith is demanding, too. But I don't think anyone is quite as demanding as Rick Pitino. Rick Pitino could also dress a player down in the best Rupp fashion. But I do think that everyone, players included, thought he did have their best interest at heart, as harsh as he could be at times on a player. I don't think there is any question that Tubby Smith has his players' best interest at heart. He shows that in every way he operates. [They're] different in style. Tubby Smith is more down home than Rick Pitino. There is not that Eastern flash, that show-business glitz and glamour.

Tom Hammond
sportscaster

If he doesn't laugh, don't you laugh. He might say something funny that you don't think is funny. But if he laughs, then you laugh.

Joe B. Hall

as a UK assistant coach to young recruit Dan Issel before the latter's first meeting with Adolph Rupp

✦ ✦ ✦

Hell, superior coaching.

Adolph Rupp

on the reason for the success of his NCAA Tournament-ineligible 1953–54 undefeated Wildcats

06

SCANDAL

*B*etween 1947 and 1950, gamblers fixed at least 86 basketball games in 33 cities throughout America, and 33 players were charged with accepting bribes to either fix games or shave points. Among them were five UK players, including three members of the Fabulous Five, who pleaded guilty to point-shaving charges. A sixth, All-America center Bill Spivey, testified before a New York grand jury that he was not involved. He later stood trial for perjury but was acquitted.

Fabulous Five members Ralph Beard, Alex Groza, and Dale Barnstable received suspended sentences. The stigma would be everlasting, ruining the professional livelihoods of Beard and Groza, both of whom had made All-NBA in 1951, the year the investigation came to light. Worst of all for Kentucky, the school was suspended by both the NCAA and SEC, and was banned from collegiate play for the 1952–53 season.

Scandal would rock UK again in 1988, when payola and academic tampering reared like a twin-headed viper.

T he scandal broke October 20, 1951, and I haven't ever forgotten it, and I won't ever forget it until they hit me in the face with that first spade full of dirt.

Ralph Beard

❊ ❊ ❊

T he gamblers couldn't touch my boys with a 10-foot pole.

Adolph Rupp

August 1951,
two months before authorities arrested three
former members of Rupp's Fabulous Five on
point-shaving charges

We just didn't think. If somebody who had suspected what was going on at Madison Square Garden had come up and told us that point shaving or things like that were against the law, we'd never have done it. Do you think we'd have jeopardized our careers—Al and Ralph, particularly, who knew they had great pro prospects—for a measly $700 or so each?

Dale Barnstable

UK forward-guard (1947–50) and
Fabulous Five member,
on the gambling scandal that shook
college basketball

⚾ ⚾ ⚾

I'm so mixed up. I wish I knew why I did it. I've been asking myself and it doesn't make sense. The money was nothing.

Ralph Beard

three days after his arrest for point-shaving,
October 1951

These guys were smooth talkers. Take you out for a stroll and treat you, and before you know it, you're into it. They point out they're not asking you to dump the game, just to pick up a few bucks by shaving a few points, but still winning and nobody getting hurt except the gamblers. And they'd ask what's wrong with going over the limit. But I'll tell you this—if those guys had offered us $10,000 or $20,000 or $30,000 to throw a game, we'd have thrown them out of the hotel window.

Dale Barnstable

Y ou take some money for winning
games, you don't know exactly what's
going on, and the next thing you know,
you are in it deep—too deep.

Dale Barnstable

● ● ●

T he undisputed facts are that he aided
and abetted in the immoral subsidiza-
tion of the players. With his knowledge, the
charges in his care were openly exploited,
their physical welfare was neglected, and
he utterly failed to build their characters or
instill any morals—indeed if he did not
impair them.

Saul S. Streit

New York General Sessions judge,
on Adolph Rupp's negligence in the
point-shaving scandal

Y ou look on yourself as a complete failure. You had blown the whole thing. You wanted to go away and die. But you don't die. You realize, finally, you can't die.

Ralph Beard

● ● ●

T o me, the biggest tragedy was Bill Spivey. He was the only guy who pleaded not guilty. He said he never took any money, and he was the only one who went to trial. He was tried on a perjury charge, and the jury was hung, something like 9 to 3, in his favor. And he was never convicted of anything. He never admitted anything, and yet he was barred from the NBA for life.

Billy Reed

At 23, basketball was the only thing I was interested in. I was going to play forever. Then, the scandal. At 23, it was like taking a wooden dagger and putting it in a vampire's heart. I figured the world was over. You could stick a fork in me, I was done.

Ralph Beard

* * *

We were beating every team in the nation, so why should I be suspicious? I never entertained the thought we were involved in the fix.

Adolph Rupp

* * *

A Kentucky player lives in a fishbowl and, when he messes up, he gets far more scrutiny than a normal student who made the same mistake.

C. M. Newton

The scandal consumed the community and the Commonwealth. This was the first time in my life that people I knew and cared about were in real trouble. It was so unbelievable. . . . Nobody will ever convince me that any of our players ever agreed to throw games. . . . I had roomed with Bill Spivey and I never had any inkling that he had any contact with gamblers. I talked with Bill and he looked me right in the eye and said, "I had nothing to do with this."

C. M. Newton

Eric Osborn, an employee at Emery Worldwide's distribution center near Los Angeles International Airport, was sorting dozens of packages when he noticed that the envelope in question had come open. The label identified the sender as Dwane Casey, who's an assistant basketball coach at the University of Kentucky. The package was addressed to Claude Mills, the father of Chris Mills, a Kentucky signee. Osborn noticed a video-cassette sticking out of the package. Then he noticed something else: 20 $50 bills.

Alexander Wolff

Sports Illustrated, *April 25, 1988,*
on the beginning of the infamous Kentucky
Shame scandal that led to heavy NCAA
sanctions against UK for recruiting and
academic violations

According to a ballot by the U.S. Basketball Writers Association, the Kentucky scandal ranked fourth among the Top 10 stories of the 1980 decade.

Jamie H. Vaught

* * *

I know I've made mistakes in my profession. I want to clean my life up. I just realized that this isn't worth it. I know wrong that has been done, and we're not going to refute that. And I know wrong that has not been done, and they're making more of a story out of that. I'm just changing. All the things that I thought were glorious and beautiful, I've come to a rude awakening that they're not.

Eddie Sutton
to close friend and former LSU head coach
Dale Brown, post-Kentucky Shame

thletics is a very competitive world. There are so many rumors and if you don't stand up and fight for yourself, you'll get swept away under the rug. You'll get taken away if you don't stand up for what's right. If you're wrong, then you expect to lose your job. But when you're right and you know you're right, and the people that you work for take the easy way out, you have to question that.

Dwane Casey

after the 1988 Emery Air Freight package scandal, in which an envelope addressed to the father of a UK recruit was found to contain $1,000. Casey, a UK assistant coach at the time, was made the scapegoat in the affair, though no hard evidence fingering him was ever found

I promise to you people in this room today, you'll see Kentucky on the cover of *Sports Illustrated* once again. And it will be cutting down certain nets.

Rick Pitino

referring to the Kentucky Shame cover story
run by the magazine in May 1989 that
eventually brought about Pitino's hiring
at Kentucky

07

MAJOR MOMENTS

I wonder if players today have the same sensation that I had. You've got to have grown up in Kentucky and to have followed the team, to have them as your heroes way before you dreamed it possible you'd be a player. I'll never forget how fortunate I was to have that opportunity, to be chosen among the many thousands of kids like me who had grown up idolizing Kentucky athletics, both football and basketball.

Joe B. Hall

I'LL TAKE MAN-HATTON

You could simply refer to them as Hatton's Heroics.

UK 1958 All-American Vernon Hatton had a knack for converting some incredible shots to win big games for Kentucky. Just ask Temple.

Back on December 7, 1957, with one second left in the first overtime, Hatton catapulted a 48-footer to tie the game, forcing a second overtime. His free throw at the end of regulation had put Kentucky into a tie with the Owls. In the third OT, Hatton was back at work, pouring in six points to give the Wildcats an 85–83 nail-biter.

Lightning struck twice for Temple later that same year, when the two clubs met again in the Final Four of the NCAA Tournament. Incredibly, Hatton beat the Owls a second time on a shot to end the game. With 16 seconds remaining and with Temple leading 60–59, Hatton scored from underneath to pull out a 61–60 Wildcats victory to advance UK to the finals against Seattle the following night.

Hatton came to play against Elgin Baylor & Co. too, scoring a game-high 30 points as Kentucky defeated Seattle 84–72 to take their fourth NCAA title.

E verywhere I go in Kentucky, people still want to talk about that shot, and that was back in 1957. It was 48 feet, 10 inches, but it gets longer every year.

Vernon Hatton

on "The Shot," December 7, 1957, vs. Temple

● ● ●

P laying on the Olympic team and getting a gold medal probably is the highlight of anybody's career. When we stood there at Wembley Stadium, they played our national anthem and we were given gold medals. I've had a lot of things to happen in sports, but I guess the Olympic Games probably would be the top notch.

Wah Wah Jones

1948 Olympic Trials final Was Greatest game ever in Madison Square Garden

After Kentucky had claimed the 1948 national championship, its first-ever NCAA crown, Coach Rupp entered his Fabulous Five in the Olympic Trials. Kentucky gained the finals—a classic against the seven-time AAU champion Phillips 66ers of Bartlesville, Oklahoma, the finest amateur team in America. Observers called it the greatest game ever played at New York's hallowed venue of sport, Madison Square Garden.

In that game, Kentucky was no match for the 66ers' seven-foot center, Bob Kurland, a former two-time consensus All-American at Oklahoma A&M. But Wildcat Ralph Beard had the game of his life, scoring 23 points. Still, UK bowed 53–49.

In an intriguing makeup of the final U.S. squad, officials named both starting fives as America's Olympic representatives.

A series of three exhibitions were played between the two teams to raise money for the Olympic Fund. The 66ers took two out of three, including a unique outdoor game played at UK's football stadium, old Stoll Field, on the University of Kentucky campus—the brainchild of Adolph Rupp, who placed a portable hardwood court over the gridiron.

M y greatest thrill had to be that Olympic team when the kids stood up there in Wembley Stadium and got their gold medals.

Adolph Rupp

M y biggest thrill came when I appeared in Alumni Gym with a UK uniform during my sophomore year [1949]. I'll never forget that moment when we went out. The band played "On, On, UK", and I thought I'd throw my first layup over the basket.

Joe B. Hall

NAILING THE
LANDMARK LAUNCHES

*T*he legendary Ralph Beard launched a 52¹/₂-foot shot to beat Tennessee in 1948. A famous photo shows Coach Rupp and the rest of the Fabulous Five gathered around Beard, as Kentucky captain Kenny Rollins drives a nail into the gym floor at the exact spot of the historic shot.

Beard's bomb erased the previous mark set, ironically, 10 years to the very day, on February 14, 1938, by two-sport star Joe "Red" Hagan, against Marquette. With just 12 seconds left and the game tied, Kentucky inbounded the ball. The clock ticked down as a pass came to Hagan, who discharged a two-hand set shot from 48 feet, 2¹/₄ inches away that ripped the net for the win. While the crowd carried Hagan off the court on its shoulders, Kentucky governor Happy Chandler sprang to the floor and asked for a nail and hammer to mark the exact spot of what was up till then the longest recorded shot in UK history.

A little over a year after Beard's shot, teammate Cliff Barker, another member of the Fabulous Five, catapulted a 65-footer against Vanderbilt, on February 26, 1949. As Barker's shot ignited the cords, UK president Dr. Herman Donovan rushed onto the court and dropped his hat where the cosmic shot originated. It is unknown if Donovan or anyone else nailed down the record breaker.

B ill Spivey was the big gun. The seven-foot "Georgia Pine" accumulated 22 points—many in the clutches. More than this point-production, however, was his terrific work under the boards. He got 21 vital rebounds—almost half of Kentucky's 45—while Kansas State got just 30.

Larry Boeck

*Louisville Courier-Journal,
on the All-America center's standout performance
in the 1951 NCAA championship game,
a 68–58 UK win*

FIDDLIN' FIVE
GIVE CARNEGIE-LIKE
PERFORMANCE

The Fiddlin' Five, a Kentucky team largely per-ceived as over-achievers, took its place along-side the Fabulous Five and other Wildcat national championship teams on March 28, 1958, at Louisville's Freedom Hall—downing Seattle 84–72 for the Big Blue's fourth national NCAA crown under Adolph Rupp.

With 16:44 left to go in the game, the Big Blue, down by six points to the Elgin Baylor-led Chieftains, began hitting from outside. Kentucky took its first lead since early in the contest with just six minutes remaining, at 61–60.

Wildcat senior All-American Vernon Hatton topped all scorers with 30 points.

Earlier in the season, Rupp had referred to his team as a bunch of fiddlers. "We've got fid-dlers, that's all. They're pretty good fiddlers — be right entertaining at a barn dance. But you need violinists to play at Carnegie Hall," he observed. "We don't have any violinists."

Though slow starting, the Fiddlin' Five closed strongly with a 19–6 regular-season mark, before streaking to four straight postseason tournament wins that earned them the coveted crown.

T he Lakers brought in the great George Mikan. And Cliff Hagan was really fired up about going against the big 6–10 center. Mikan was considered the best player in pro basketball at the time and even though he was six inches taller than Cliff, Cliff was quicker. He completely outplayed Mikan.

Gayle Rose
*Wildcat player (1952, 1954–55),
on one of the two games UK played against
the NBA's Minneapolis Lakers in 1952–53, the
season Kentucky was banned from playing
NCAA basketball*

O ne of my happiest moments was during that season when we were ranked No. 2 and Vanderbilt was ranked third in the country. We went down there to play for more or less the conference champi-onship. I had my best game as a college player. I still have the audio tape of that game with Cawood Ledford calling it. I lis-ten to that every once in a while because it's something I can relive through the eyes and the voice of someone else.

Louie Dampier
*who scored a career-high 42 points
on February 2, 1966, in a 105–90 UK victory
over the Commodores*

The best moment I remember is the game at Ole Miss when I broke the single-game record and became the all-time leading scorer at Kentucky, and the reason it meant so much to me is my dad. My father each year would go on one or two trips so that by the end of my senior year he would have visited every town in the Southeastern Conference. It just happened to work out that he was at Ole Miss.

Dan Issel

FAST BREAK: During his senior season, Issel scored at least 40 points six different times and tallied at least 50 points twice.

One of the finest was in 1975 in Dayton Arena in the finals of the Mideast Region against undefeated Indiana, ranked number one in the nation. They had beaten us by 24 points in Bloomington earlier in December. That comeback win, which put us in the Final Four in San Diego, was probably the most exciting game I've ever been a part of, even the national finals.

Joe B. Hall

● ● ●

All the Kentucky tradition, all the history, and all the spirits of past players won that game. I really believe that.

Joe B. Hall
on the 94–93 overtime win over Mississippi State
in 1976 that closed out the Memorial Coliseum era.
Hall gave the game ball to Adolph Rupp,
then in his fourth year of retirement

Givens played the finest game of any player I've ever played against.

Jim Spanarkle
Duke guard,
on Jack Givens's 41-point performance in the
1978 NCAA championship game

My shot was dropping, so I just kept shooting. At one time in the second half, I took one shot that hit the side of the backboard and went in. I was really ready. I never felt better before a game than I did tonight.

Jack Givens
on his 1978 NCAA title game
MVP performance

GOOSE GOES WILD
IN '78 TITLE GAME

It was Jack "Goose" Givens's night, and what a farewell to Big Blue basketball it was for the then-No. 2 all-time scorer in Wildcat history.

Before 18,721 at the Checkerdome in St. Louis, Givens burned the nets for 41 points, the third highest individual scoring total ever in an NCAA title game, behind UCLA's Bill Walton (44 pts. in 1973) and Gail Goodrich (42 pts., 1965). His performance highlighted Kentucky's 94–88 NCAA finals triumph over Duke for the Cats' fifth national championship and first under Coach Joe B. Hall.

The turning point came with just 57 seconds to play in the first half. Two Mike Gminski free throws had cut UK's lead to a single point. But Givens single-handedly extended the Wildcats' advantage to seven at the half, with six straight unanswered points. He wound up canning 18 of 27 from the floor.

For Hall, the crown meant relief from the suffocating weight of Adolph Rupp's legacy.

"The pressure's been on for six seasons, really," confirmed Hall.

En route to the title, Kentucky also claimed its 31st SEC championship.

"There's no finer way to go out," said Givens.

Certainly, the most memorable game to me was the Duke game in St. Louis when we won the championship. That one will always have a warm spot in my heart. Not necessarily because it was the best game we played, but because it was the most important in my career while I was at Kentucky.

Joe B. Hall

ANDERSON, MACY MIRACLES
MOW DOWN KANSAS

*T*railing by six points with just 31 seconds to go in overtime, Kentucky's Mr. Cool, Kyle Macy, and freshman Dwight Anderson tallied seven points between them to rally the 10th-ranked Wildcats to a stirring 67–66 triumph over previously undefeated and fifth-ranked Kansas, on December 9, 1978, in Lexington.

The OT heroics began when Anderson canned a bucket plus two free throws to cut the Jayhawks' lead to two. The freshman ace, playing like a seasoned veteran, then knocked Kansas' inbounds pass out of the hands of KU's Mac Stallcup, somehow managing to swat the ball across court to teammate Kyle Macy with just 10 seconds left. Macy then routinely hit a 15-footer with four seconds remaining to tie the game.

Kansas hurriedly called a timeout but was assessed a technical foul for having already used its one allotted timeout in overtime. Macy then sank the winning free throw, though Kentucky hearts palpitated as the ball hit the front end of the rim before finally falling in.

"The effort to make seven points in 31 seconds is almost unbelievable," said Wildcats coach Joe B. Hall. "But I felt all during the game we could win."

D on't forget that wintry day when Rex Chapman guided the Wildcats to a stunning 85–51 victory over defending national champion Louisville in a nationally televised matchup at Freedom Hall. The 6–5 freshman pumped in a game-high 26 points, including five three-pointers. His performance resulted in a lot of national press, including a cover story by noted writer Curry Kirkpatrick in *Sports Illustrated.*

Jamie H. Vaught

● ● ●

W e could have wound up with Noriega. UK about pushed us out of the continent early.

Dale Brown
*LSU head coach,
on UK's 100–95 upset win over LSU,
February 15, 1990*

D uke's 104–103 overtime triumph over Kentucky in the East Regional championship game was won by Grant Hill's 75-foot-plus pass and Christian Laettner's 17-foot buzzer-beater. There was evidence all around that the final, stunning 2.1 second climax—and the passionate two and a half hours that built to the decisive basket—belonged among the most gripping moments of theater in the 54-year history of the tournament; and for that matter, in the century since James Naismith came up with a very good idea.

Malcolm Moran
New York Times,
March 29, 1992

We were just screaming and yelling when we got back to the dressing room. It was a big win for us. We had come back from 31 points down and had lost two in a row going into that game. We were giving each other high fives. We just could not believe what we had done. It's something I know I'll always remember.

Jeff Brassow

*UK player (1990–91, 1993–94),
on the greatest comeback in UK history—
the 99–95 win over LSU, February 15, 1994*

● ● ●

It's the proudest moment of my coaching life.

Rick Pitino

*on rallying from a 19-point deficit in
regulation—then from nine behind in
overtime—to edge defending national
champion Arkansas, 95–93, in the 1995
SEC Tournament final*

Make it two thumbs up for *Die Hard 3* [Kentucky-Arkansas, 1995 SEC finals], a spine-tingling sequel from the producers of *The Greatest Game Ever Played* [Kentucky-Duke, 1992 East Regional finals] and *The Greatest Comeback Ever Made* [UK beats LSU in 1994, after being down 31 points with 15:34 to play]. The three scripts share a preposterous central plot that is beyond even Steven Spielberg's wildest hoop dreams.

Mark Coomes
Louisville Courier-Journal,
March 12, 1995

● ● ●

Call it Coronation by Committee.

Rick Bozich
*on UK's team-wide contribution in gaining
the 1998 NCAA crown*

I couldn't watch any more. My nerves couldn't take it. But I could tell by the roar of the crowd that it was a great game.

C. M. Newton

*on the nail-biting conclusion of the Cats' 1998
NCAA championship game win over Utah*

❋ ❋ ❋

I t's like putting Frank Sinatra and the Rolling Stones on the same stage and calling it a warmup act.

Mark Woods

*writer/columnist,
on the pre-game buildup to Kentucky-UCLA
in the 1998 NCAA South Regional, taken anti-
climactically by the Wildcats, 94–68.
The game was a prelude to an even more
hyped matchup with Duke that followed in the
regional finals*

We knew we would comeback. We are the comeback kids.

Tubby Smith

after his Wildcats won the NCAA title in 1998, Smith's first season as UK head coach

* * *

Now the state is in seventh heaven. Three years, three trips to the title game, two championships.

Mark Woods

on Kentucky's run through the NCAA Tournament from 1996 through '98, in which UK won its sixth and seventh national championships

R emember the Alamodome.

Pat Forde

*on the site of Kentucky's seventh NCAA crown,
in 1998*

● ● ●

T he No Star Team is the toast of the
Lone Star State.

Pat Forde

*on the 1998 national champion Wildcats,
the team without a star player*

I knew I was having a really good night, but not until I heard the crowd chanting, "We want 40," did I know I was really that close.

Tayshaun Prince
forward (1999–2002)/
SEC Player of the Year (2001),
on his career-high 41-point performance
in UK's second-round win over Tulsa in the
2002 NCAA Tournament

● ● ●

We caught fire. Anywhere in the gym tonight, Sparks was going to hit it.

Chuck Hayes
forward (2002–05),
on teammate Patrick Sparks's output against
Alabama to help clinch the 2005 SEC title
for Kentucky, the Cats' 43rd SEC championship.
In all UK hit on 13 of 19 three-pointers, with
Sparks connecting on seven of them and
amassing 26 points in the Wildcats' 78–71
victory at Tuscaloosa. Late in the first half,
Kentucky trailed by as many as 14 points

Sparks's shot, which dramatically bounced once, twice, three times on the rim before falling through, completed a Kentucky rally from an eight-point deficit in the final eight minutes of regulation.

Steve Wieberg
USA TODAY
on the Cats' near-miraculous comeback in the 94–88 double-overtime loss to Michigan State in the 2005 NCAA Austin Regional

Patrick Sparks made the most dramatic shot of the 2005 tournament—and, arguably, the most dramatic shot in the impossibly rich history of Kentucky basketball. And it still wasn't enough to stop on-a-mission Michigan State.

Pat Forde
ESPN.com

When you go to the replay and you first see it, the camera angles that you have are very difficult. And I felt the play was so important in deciding a college basketball game that was as great as that, I asked the guy in the truck to blow it up for me. I don't know how many angles he had, but he showed me every single angle he possibly could and I still really couldn't find anything that would overrule my original decision.

Jim Burr

the referee who signaled that UK's Patrick Sparks's desperation three-pointer at the end of regulation was good, sending the 2005 NCAA Austin Regional final against Michigan State into eventual double overtime

KENTUCKY
WILDCATS
ALL-TIME TEAM

*N*othing in all of UK hoops history, not even the legendary Baron himself, generates as much excitement as the great players that have worn the Blue and White. Apparently Coach Rupp stopped far short of picking anything resembling an all-time team for his Wildcats. That won't stop us, but it's a Herculean undertaking.

Author Dave Kindred wrote that Rupp once described the perfect Kentucky player—an entity with "the shooting eye of Larry Pursiful and Louie Dampier, the drive of Frank Ramsey, the speed of Ralph Beard and Ronnie Lyons, the grace of Cliff Hagan, the defensive ability of Billy Evans and Kenny Rollins, the temperament of Aggie Sale, the rebounding ability of Bob Burrow, the passing wizardry of Cliff Barker, the competitive spirit of Wah Wah Jones, the scholastic ability of Jim McDonald, the hands of Cotton Nash, and the scoring ability of Dan Issel."

Sign that guy up!

CLIFF HAGAN

forward (1951–52, '54)

two-time consensus All-America (1952, '54),
two-time All-SEC (1952, '54),
Basketball Hall of Fame (1977),
UK athletic director (1975–88)

● ● ●

Cliff Hagan was a player who seemed to have rehearsed every move he made on the court, he did things with such ease. Rupp said Hagan had the "best touch of any player I ever coached." Hagan knew precisely how hard to put the ball on the backboard. With that touch, he had good timing and exceptional jumping ability.

Tev Laudeman

JAMAL MASHBURN

forward (1991–93)

two-time All-SEC (1992, '93),
consensus All-America (1993),
co-SEC Player of the Year (1993),
All-NCAA Tournament team (1993)

● ● ●

The single-most important Wildcat in the post-probation era. . . . He was the athlete, the complete basketball player that Pitino needed to help kick-start the program and the recruiting process. Could score, pass, rebound, and defend.

Tom Wallace
on Mashburn

DAN ISSEL

center (1968–70)

two-time All-America (1969–70),
three-time All-SEC (1968–70),
UK student-athlete of the year (1970),
All-NCAA Tournament team, regional (1968–70)

⚾ ⚾ ⚾

If you want sheer production, Issel is your man. . . . He is Kentucky's all-time leading scorer and career leader in rebounds. . . . A bruising interior player, he sometimes lags behind on the UK honor roll because he didn't play on a national championship team.

Michael Bradley

RALPH BEARD

point guard (1946–49)

three-time consensus All-America (1947–49),
member 1948 gold medal-winning
U.S. Olympic Basketball Team,
four-time All-SEC Tournament selection (1946–49),
played on two NCAA national championship
teams (1948, '49)

⚾ ⚾ ⚾

When Beard ran, you could smell the rubber burning.

Adolph Rupp

⚾ ⚾ ⚾

If not for the point-shaving scandal, the glory that was Bob Cousy's may well have come to Beard. As contemporaries in college and then in the NBA—Beard was a second-year pro when Cousy was a rookie—Beard was always superior.

Dave Kindred

LOUIE DAMPIER

shooting guard (1965–67)

two-time All-SEC (1966, '67),
All-NCAA Final Four team (1966),
two-time Academic All-America (1966, '67)

● ● ●

The runt of the litter on the undersized 1966 Wildcats, Louie Dampier was the best pure shooter in the storied history of Kentucky basketball. Time and again, he let fly from far out in the pre–3-point shot era. Still he knocked down 50.8 percent of his field-goal attempts. . . . He then became an American Basketball Association legend with the Kentucky Colonels, finishing as the league's all-time leading scorer.

Michael Bradley

ADOLPH RUPP

coach (1931–72)

four NCAA national championships
(1948, '49, '51, '58);
one NIT championship (1946);
27 Southeastern Conference titles;
retired as winningest coach in the history of college
basketball (876), a mark that stood for 25 years;
four-time National Coach of the Year,
Basketball Hall of Fame (1969)

※ ※ ※

H e was a Patton on the basketball floor.

Dickie Parsons

※ ※ ※

S ome guys say they hated Rupp. Not me.
He was it as far as I was concerned. If
he told me to run through a brick wall, I'd
have backed up as far as it would take.

Ralph Beard

KENTUCKY WILDCATS
ALL-TIME TEAM

FIRST TEAM

Cliff Hagan *(1951–52, '54), forward*
Jamal Mashburn *(1991–93), forward*
Dan Issel *(1968–70), center*
Ralph Beard *(1946–49), point guard*
Louie Dampier *(1965–67), shooting guard*

Adolph Rupp *(1931–72), coach*

SECOND TEAM

Cotton Nash *(1962–64), forward*
Kevin Grevey *(1973–75), forward*
Alex Groza *(1945, 1947–49), center*
Kyle Macy *(1978–80), guard*
Frank Ramsey *(1951–52, '54), guard*

Rick Pitino *(1990–97), coach*

09

THE GREAT KENTUCKY FIVES

I guess maybe I got hooked up with Johnny Cox's 1958 national championship team during that time because Johnny was from Hazard [Kentucky] and played real tough basketball. But I followed and enjoyed all of them. We've had some good players, and the Cotton Nash group was good. I didn't get to see the 1951 and '52 teams play as much but the Frank Ramsey group was a great group. We were playing in the NBA at the same time and didn't get to see them as much as I wanted to. Louie Dampier and his group, and Kyle Macy. We had so many good groups. It's hard to pick one out.

Wah Wah Jones

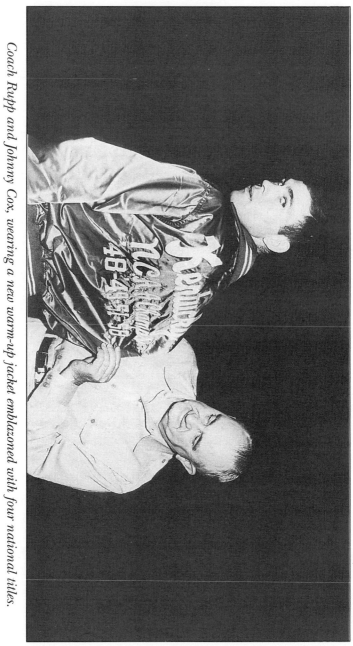

Coach Rupp and Johnny Cox, wearing a new warm-up jacket emblazoned with four national titles.

AP/Wide World Photos

Mississippi State saw more blue uniforms than their granddads did in 1861.

Ralph McGill
Atlanta writer,
on the 1933 Cats, who claimed the
SEC Tournament final, 46–27

● ● ●

It will take a feat of magic to beat Old Kaintuck. The droll and delightful Col. Rupp, suh, is more heavily loaded than a moonshiner's shotgun. He has all-American players picking up splinters on his bench and one such operative quit the squad in disgust because he couldn't even make the second team.

Arthur Daley
New York Times,
March 24, 1947

J oe Lapchick called them the greatest team he had ever coached against. The Associated Press said they were "the greatest aggregation to visit the Eighth Avenue arena [Madison Square Garden]."

Russell Rice
on the 1946–47 Wildcats

* * *

I t was the Fabulous Five era—I was the eighth of the Five.

Joe B. Hall
*on his playing days at UK during the reign of
one of college basketball's greatest ensembles
ever, in the late 1940s*

P atton's Third Army freed Cliff Barker from a German prisoner-of-war camp; the army nurtured and developed Alex Groza into one of the finest pivot men ever to wear the Kentucky colors; and the navy matured Kenny Rollins into a fine floor leader. Beard was perhaps the most idolized of the group. In training all year round, he was described by the school annual as "the perfect Wheaties ad, the All-American boy." Jones was dubbed "Wah Wah" because as a child a younger sister could not pronounce his name.

Russell Rice
on the Fabulous Five

The Wildcats became the second quintet to win both the NCAA and National Invitation Tournament crowns, tying Utah, who was the first to accomplish this feat, in 1944.

Larry Boeck

Louisville Courier-Journal,
on the 1948 Kentucky team

● ● ●

The Fabulous Five—known individually as guards Ralph Beard and Kenny Rollins, center Alex Groza, and forwards Cliff Barker and Wallace "Wah Wah" Jones—was not only the best, it was the first to burn the word "Kentucky" into the consciousness of American sport. If UK is truly the Roman Empire of college basketball, then Rupp and his renowned quintet are Romulus and Remus.

Mark Coomes

Of all the achievement-filled seasons during this period probably the greatest was 1947–48, the season of UK's most famous team, the "Fabulous Five." The Wildcats not only posted a 36–3 record and held the conference title and their first NCAA championship, but also provided half of the U.S. Olympic Basketball Team which went on to win a gold medal at the Olympic Games in London.

Bert Nelli
Steve Nelli

* * *

The ball might touch the court once or twice but never more. None of this dribble, dribble, dribble. It was bing, bing and in it went.

Harry Lancaster
on how the Fabulous Five ran the fast break

We had the killer instinct. I get so disturbed with teams that get fifteen- or so point leads at halftime and fritter it away in the second half. Brother, if we got twenty on a ball club that was just the beginning. We weren't satisfied. We wanted twenty more and more often than not we got them. No mercy! None whatsoever. We never had compassion for anyone.

Kenny Rollins
guard (1943, '47, '48),
on the Fabulous Five of 1948

* * *

Rupp would never admit it but that was the best team we had man for man.

Harry Lancaster
on the 1948, '49 Fabulous Five

T hey were a beautiful team. They had the finest fast break I have ever seen, before or since. It was just magnificent the way Alex Groza got the ball off the board.

Harry Lancaster
on the Fabulous Five:
1948, '49 NCAA champions

● ● ●

H ow many college teams could go into the pros now as a franchise and hold their own?

Ralph Beard
on the singular achievement of the Fabulous
Five, selected for the 1948 Olympic gold medal-
winning team, and then by the NBA,
as the Indianapolis Olympians franchise
from 1950 through '52

FAST BREAK: *Fabulous Five member Kenny Rollins played three years in the NBA, but not with Indianapolis.*

I have always felt that the 1951 team was the forgotten team among the six NCAA Championship teams. I don't know if it was overshadowed by the investigation and later punishment of the school for the players' involvement in the point-shaving scandal, but for some reason that team just never received the notoriety of the other five champions.

Cawood Ledford
in 1997

❋ ❋ ❋

The bunch regarded as fiddlers—Rupp had said he needed violinists for a "Carnegie Hall schedule"—ended the season blissfully and sounding like Heifetz playing Brahms on a Stradavarius.

Larry Boeck
*on the Fiddlin' Five of '58, who brought
Kentucky its fourth national crown*

A child of the 1970s recently came upon a photograph of the 1966 University of Kentucky basketball team. She studied the players' snug-fitting blazers with the tiny lapels, their white shirts, and dry-look hairstyles. A flicker of amusement crossed her face as she announced, "They look like the Beatles."

C. Ray Hall
Louisville Courier-Journal,
March 30, 1986

● ● ●

These boys are coachable. They listen and they do what they're supposed to. They're a pleasure and they're all regular. They are regular to the last man. It would be mean if they lost a game.

Adolph Rupp
on his Rupp's Runts of 1965–66

When they lost the national championship game [in 1966], grief covered Kentucky from Pineville to Paducah. Somehow that team had worked its way so deeply into the state's psyche that losing a basketball game seemed like losing a life.

C. Ray Hall

❀ ❀ ❀

Maybe that's the way we'll go down in history. Maybe we had a hand in the Emancipation Proclamation of 1966.

Pat Riley

*on the 1966 NCAA championship game
(all-black Texas Western vs. all-white
Kentucky), which forever changed the makeup
of college basketball*

They were like five guys who make their living sledge-hammering steers in a stockyard.

Anonymous Chicago sportswriter
*who dubbed the UK team of 1975
the Slaughterhouse Five*

⚾ ⚾ ⚾

We're real this year.

Jimmy Dan Conner
1975 team's spiritual leader

⚾ ⚾ ⚾

This team is one of the finest teams I have seen in my lifetime, and they could blow out some of my national championship teams.

Adolph Rupp
*on Joe B. Hall's 1975 Wildcat team that made
it to the NCAA finals in San Diego,
before bowing to UCLA in Bruins coach
John Wooden's last game*

They're awesome. I can see why they're No. 1. They have a lot of smart personnel and their power is unlimited.

Darrell Hedric

*former Miami of Ohio head coach,
on the 1978 Cats*

I believe it is an advantage that the players were in the Final Four as freshmen. They remember the thrill of being there. This time they want to win. These seniors have been a lot of places. The confidence that they have has to be a big help.

Joe B. Hall

on his 1978 NCAA national champions

Best team I ever look.

Alexander Gomelsky
*USSR head coach,
on the Kentucky Wildcats, after UK had
obliterated his Soviet National Team, 109–75,
at Memorial Coliseum in November 1977.
The Wildcats would go on to become
national champions*

⚾ ⚾ ⚾

When you can shoot 38 percent and
you win, you know you're a great
defensive team.

Rick Pitino
*on his Kentucky team's performance in the
1996 NCAA finals against Syracuse. UK's
38.4 scoring percentage was the lowest for a
champion in 33 years. On the defensive end,
the Wildcats forced 24 Orange turnovers*

After winning its three tournament games by an average of 22 points, No. 7 Kentucky put four players on the All-Tournament team—the first time one team had such a monopoly since the 1947 UK team.

Mark Woods

Louisville Courier-Journal,
on the 1998 SEC tourney and
national champion Wildcats

Fifty years after Adolph Rupp and his Fabulous Five gave Kentucky its first NCAA title, Tubby Smith and his modern-day Wildcats put together a story that will join the original in Bluegrass folklore.

Mark Woods

on the 1998 Wildcats

We realize what got us here. It's team-work.

Jeff Sheppard
guard (1994–98)/1998 Final Four
Most Outstanding Player,
on the 1998 national champions

❋ ❋ ❋

Looking at this modest UK team next to its heroic accomplishments is like looking at the ancient Egyptians next to their pyramids. How did they do it?

Pat Forde
on the '98 Kentucky team

Everybody has said and written all year that there aren't any superstars or All-Americans on this team. And they're right. We don't have any superstars. But we really have a lot of guys who really learned how to sacrifice and make each other better as a team. And that's the reason that we won this championship.

Scott Padgett
on the 1998 national champion Wildcats

If this team lacked superstars—and it did—the Wildcats more than made up for it with a team concept that emphasized role players.

Michael Bradley
on the 1998 Comeback Cats

While the 1997/98 edition of Wild-cats did not win artistically, it somehow managed to win. And win. First one player would rise to the challenge, and then in the next game, someone else. While fans and the media noted that the Big Blue exhibited neither form nor finesse, Coach Smith could have pointed out to them that in a basketball game points are not awarded on the basis of appearance.

Bert Nelli
Steve Nelli

I t's a sign of a team with heart, when you can win like we did.

Tubby Smith

*on his 2005 Cats,
who edged Ole Miss 53–50 in mid-January
at Oxford after trailing by 15 points. UK had
similarly overcome a 16-point deficit to defeat
Louisville, 60–58, the previous month*

❋ ❋ ❋

I t makes us feel great to be remembered in the same area like the Fiddlin' Five, even Rupp's Runts although they never won the championship; the Unbelievables; the Untouchables; and then the Comeback Cats. There is something neat about playing at a school where the successful teams are given a name or a positive nickname at the end of the season.

Cameron Mills

ROYAL COURTS
OF BLUE

*T*he four lairs of Kentucky Wildcats basketball all yield a storied past.

Some followers of the Big Blue might assume that Wildcat roots began at Alumni Gym. In fact, Alumni, the "first house that Rupp built," was inaugurated in 1924. Before that, UK crammed its followers into the old gym in Barker Hall's Buell Armory, a place deemed unsafe for even the few people it could hold.

But it was there that Kentucky basketball took flight, hosting UK home games for 22 seasons, from 1903 through the 1923–24 campaign. It was also where Kentucky's first All-American, forward Basil Hayden, showcased his talents while captaining the 1920–21 squad that went 13–1 and was crowned Southern Intercollegiate champion.

Despite a meager 134–108–1 overall mark at Buell Armory, consistently large crowds had to be turned away from the tiny facility. Finally, with murmurings that the state high school tournament might soon withdraw from the antiquated site, the school's Board of Trustees quickly moved, in 1923, to approve a new home for Kentucky hoops.

O nce spectators got in that old gym we played in, there was hardly room to play the game. And I remember the poles that held up the running track that ran around the top of the gym. We always had to dodge those things.

George Buchheit
coach (1919–24),
on Kentucky's first home court, the old
Gymnasium (later the Ladies' Gym) in Barker
Hall, which housed about 650 spectators for
Wildcat home games through 1924

❋ ❋ ❋

A lumni Gym, the 2,800-seat, red-brick structure dating to 1924, couldn't accommodate even the students, whose tickets were rationed; a student got to see every third game.

C. Ray Hall

ALUMNI GYM

Completed for play in time for the 1924–25 season, Alumni Gym, seating a robust 2,800 spectators, ushered in the golden age of UK basketball.

In the 271 games played there over 26 seasons, between 1924 and 1950, the Wildcats lost just 24 times. Six seasons after opening its doors, the $100,000 facility welcomed the incomparable age of Rupp basketball. During its legendary tenure at the corner of the Avenue of Champions and South Limestone, Alumni Gym hosted the era of the Fabulous Five—the most brilliant as well as the darkest period in UK annals.

By 1948, Alumni had swollen to a 4,000-seat capacity, but it wasn't nearly enough to satisfy the demand for tickets. Rupp saluted the old gym with a magnificent extended farewell, closing down the house with 84 consecutive victories—a string that ran for more than seven seasons, from January 4, 1943, through the gym's finale against Vanderbilt, on February 25, 1950.

T alk about your homecourt advantage. From the minute the Wildcats moved into Alumni Gym, opponents found it next to impossible to win there. Kentucky put together a remarkable 247–24 record over 26 seasons at the gym, capping its success with an 84-game home winning streak. Adolph Rupp's teams were 203–8 in 20 seasons there.

Michael Bradley

⊛ ⊛ ⊛

O ld-timers will tell you that the new building [Rupp Arena] doesn't match the atmosphere of Memorial Coliseum. The character of great tradition permeates the air with near spiritual force, even today, as the building serves as the Wildcats' primary practice facility.

2004–05 Kentucky Basketball Media Guide

MEMORIAL COLISEUM

Memorial Coliseum opened its arms in the fall of 1950 and immediately embraced a champion—Kentucky would win its third NCAA Championship in Memorial's maiden year, the school's third national crown in four seasons.

Many thought the Memorial project to be a "white elephant," because basketball was still perceived by many as just a wintertime respite between football and baseball. The facility, seating 11,500, continued the venerable homecourt-winning streak begun at old Alumni Gym in 1943. For more than 12 years in all, the Cats kept it up, emerging victorious 129 consecutive times, an NCAA record that still stands to this day, with the last 45 games of that historic run played at Memorial.

The block-long fortress, built as a memorial to the 10,000 Kentuckians who lost their lives during World War II, still serves today as the practice facility for the Wildcats. They say the old place has retained its spirit, and who in Blue would doubt that the wraiths of Spivey, Hagan, Ramsey, Burrow, Hatton, Cox, Nash, Dampier, Riley, Issel, Grevey, Conner, and Givens don't all run the court in a ghostly pickup game in the wee hours on game nights?

M emorial Coliseum, a brick-and-mortar symbol of the program's great tradition, was a snake pit for opposing teams. Adolph Rupp's Wildcats won their first 45 games at the facility, and in 25 seasons there, Kentucky posted seven perfect home records, lost only one game eight times and fashioned a 306–38 mark overall.

Michael Bradley

* * *

T he main thing [about Rupp Arena] is how much different it is from Memorial Coliseum; how many more people there are and how much more elaborate everything is. I say to myself, "Look at all of these people in this big arena and how things have changed in 20 years."

Louie Dampier

RUPP ARENA

Cavernous, hexagonal Rupp Arena enveloped Wildcat basketball in 1976 and offers exactly twice the number of seats as Memorial Coliseum to Blue and White zealots desiring to view their Cats.

The Rupp is divided into two seating areas: the upper and lower levels, with 13,000 in the high altitudes, 10,000 at sea level. Kentucky wins here at about the same clip as it did in Memorial—hovering near 90 percent.

The massive structure is part of the $53 million Lexington Center complex, which houses a convention-exhibition center, in addition to a tri-level enclosed shopping mall and a major hotel.

It is fitting that after having "built" two previous basketball houses, a facility of this enormous magnitude should be named after Adolph Rupp.

The Cats of course make an annual trek to Louisville, and there's some nice history there as well. The school first played in the Derby City in 1908, just five years after the inception of Kentucky basketball. The Freedom Hall era began in 1957–58 and was the site that same season of the Big Blue's fourth NCAA championship.

Rupp, which opened in November 1976, remains one of college basketball's most impressive venues. . . . UK's home records there include marks of 18–0, 16–0 [three times] 15–0, 14–0, and 13–0 [twice]. Kentucky has won three national championships since moving into Rupp.

Michael Bradley

❋ ❋ ❋

Kentucky puts SRO—23,000 people—in Rupp Arena; if they built an arena seating 50,000, there would still be a waiting list.

Al McGuire

WINNING
AND LOSING

I t was the first time most of the fans in the gym ever had seen a Kentucky team beaten.

Ed Ashford

Lexington Herald/Louisville Courier-Journal,
on the stunning loss to a below-average
Georgia Tech team at Memorial Coliseum,
January 8, 1955, which ended the Cats'
129-game homecourt winning streak
dating back to January 2, 1943

I've never believed in moral victories. I don't think playing a highly ranked team to a six- or eight-point loss helps your ball club. I think you have to play to win.

Rick Pitino

● ● ●

The eternal verity in Rupp's personality was his love of victory.

Dave Kindred

● ● ●

They say Kentucky goes as Beard goes. Last night he just didn't go.

Louis Effrat

New York Times,
March 24, 1947,
on Ralph Beard's poorest performance as a
Wildcat—a one-point effort in UK's 49–45 loss
to Utah in the finals of the 1947 NIT
at Madison Square Garden

He would not accept defeat, and he didn't want anybody that played for him to accept defeat. And it always killed him, as it did us.

Ralph Beard
on Adolph Rupp

* * *

I don't know how there could be any additional pressure. They [fans] do expect us to win every game, but these problems have always been at Kentucky. I'd hate for it to get to the point where it wasn't.

Joe B. Hall

* * *

There is not a team sport on any level that wins consistently without good, solid defense. That's the stabilizing force in your program. Defense is more consistent than offense. You have bad shooting nights, but defense can remain consistent.

Eddie Sutton

We were winning. Every year we would maybe lose two, three or four games. . . . We knew what it took to get the job done and we tried to play the game like it was supposed to be played and help each other out. I think that's the secret to it.

Wah Wah Jones

* * *

I can't remember the last time I didn't score in double figures, but this team is filled with guys who went out and got 30 a night in high school. I'm not the only one making sacrifices.

Sam Bowie

* * *

I'm not engaged in a popularity contest. I want to win basketball games.

Adolph Rupp

I t was a violent game. I don't mean there were any fights—but they were desperate, and they were committed, and they were more motivated than we were. They were playing for identity, for respect. They were angry, and we weren't. They had more passion and commitment.

Pat Riley
on the 1966 Texas Western Miners

● ● ●

L osing . . . that year was possibly the biggest disappointment of my life, because that was my best coaching job.

Adolph Rupp
on the national championship game loss to Texas Western in 1966

● ● ●

I don't think he ever recovered emotionally.

Dan Issel
on Adolph Rupp after the Texas Western loss

Title Game Loss
to Miners Had Civil,
Social Implications

It was more than just an NCAA championship game.

When Kentucky squared off against Texas Western in the finals of the national title game, on March 19, 1966, at College Park, Maryland, the game extended way beyond the parameters of the action on the court—it was a matter of black and white: Texas Western's starting all-black five against Kentucky's all-white cast of Rupp's Runts.

Many say the Runts would've been the Baron's favorite team had the Wildcats won that night. But the Miners were a talented and unusually motivated team, carrying not only the mantel of Texas Western (now Texas-El Paso) but the hopes of an entire race on their collective backs, as integration began to slowly sweep across the landscape of Southern sports in the mid-Sixties.

The underdog Miners sank 28-of-34 free throws en route to stunning the world, as they upset the Big Blue, 72–65.

We're probably better known for losing that game than we would be if we'd won.

Larry Conley
starting forward, Rupp's Runts,
on the 1966 NCAA championship game loss

● ● ●

It was basketball's most fantastic and dramatic upset. . . . Few people here can believe yet what unfolded before their startled eyes.

Larry Boeck
Louisville Courier-Journal,
on Kentucky's opening-round loss to Loyola
in the 1949 NIT—one of the games, it was
subsequently revealed, that was involved in the
infamous point-shaving scandal

● ● ●

They had fun. They just didn't show it. They couldn't show it. Coach Rupp wouldn't allow it.

C. M. Newton
on the late-1940s national championship teams
at Kentucky

We beat a team that had three NBA draft picks on it and we went into the game believing we would win it. I think our fans started believing that we were going to definitely build the program back up. There's no question about it, that win over LSU was the benchmark in our rebuilding program.

Rick Pitino

on UK's 100–95 upset of LSU, February 15, 1990

● ● ●

We weren't ready to go home. We feel like we've got something to defend here. We want to end our careers on a high note. W just willed ourselves to win.

Scott Padgett

on UK's 92–88 overtime win over Kansas in the second-round of the NCAA Midwest Regional, March 14, 1999

Keep 'em close, boys, and I'll think of something.

Adolph Rupp

● ● ●

You live for games like this, ones that are memorable. But those are the ones that also cause heartache and are painful forever.

Jeff Sheppard
after edging Duke, 86–84, in the 1998 NCAA South Region finals to advance to the Final Four. Sheppard scored 18 points in the big win

● ● ●

Everyone was expecting us to win, and we did.

Jeff Sheppard
on the 1996 national championship Wildcats, who dunked Syracuse in the NCAA finals, 76–67, behind Tony Delk's six-of-seven three-point shooting in the first half

J oe B. Hall did something many coaches who follow famous men fail to do—he started winning. He started winning his way, with his players.

Rick Bozich

❋ ❋ ❋

C ollege basketball writers expected Kentucky to win the national title. Opposing coaches liked the Wildcats, too. Expectations raged within UK fans. In a situation where greatness was expected, greatness is what Joe B. Hall demanded. Sometimes winning when you are expected to win can be the most difficult coaching assignment in sports.

Rick Bozich

There was The Loss. The one people will be talking about for decades. . . . March 28, 1992. The East Regional in Philadelphia. Kentucky vs. Duke. That, of course, was the game Christian Laettner took a length-of-the-court inbounds pass from Grant Hill, spun around at the top of the key, and fired up a jump shot over two UK defenders. If the home run that Bobby Thomson hit to send the Giants to the 1951 World Series was "The Shot Heard 'Round the World," then the 17-footer that propelled Duke into the 1992 Final Four was "The Shot Seen 'Round the World."

Mark Woods

What about the losses? There were only 50 of them in eight years. But they often were spectacular. And in their own way, they usually were more revealing than any victory.

Mark Woods
on the Pitino era in Lexington

● ● ●

Winning was what mattered to the Baron of the Bluegrass. The Comeback Cats and their coach had become a vital part of that tradition.

Bert Nelli
Steve Nelli
on the 1998 NCAA champions

● ● ●

It will go down in history as a great college basketball game. It hurts right now, but some of our guys will appreciate it later on.

Tubby Smith
on the double-overtime loss to Michigan State in the 2005 NCAA Tournament

12

BITTER FOES

*D*uke, Louisville, Indiana . . . mere mention of the names stirs fire in the hearts of Kentuckians.

The Wildcats enjoy the rarity of a big-time national program that transcends the usual local or regional rivalry (Louisville excluded). In other words, Kentucky basketball is so huge, its bitterest rivals are national foes.

Former Cat coach Rick Pitino once said, "Anytime you are at Kentucky, people are going to be jealous because we have the best fans, the best facilities, the best tradition. . . . You can't worry about the jealous people. That is a part of life."

And so it is. Rivalries are a two-way street. Somewhere, be it Durham, Bloomington, Louisville or other center of hoop madness, fans feel the same way about the Big Blue as Kentucky fans feel about them.

We respect 'em, but we don't fear 'em.

Richie Farmer
*guard (1989–92),
on the Duke Blue Devils, before Kentucky's
memorable 104–103 loss in the East Regional
final—"the Greatest Game Ever Played,"
March 28, 1992*

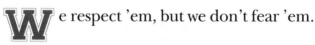

It was the most physical game I ever played in, bar none, and I played 10 years in the NBA. I can't remember a game I played in at Kentucky that was as important or where we had more at stake.

Kevin Grevey
*on the 92–90 win over top-ranked Indiana in
the 1975 Mideast Regional final, after being
annihilated by the Hoosiers, 98–74, earlier
in the season*

It was the biggest win in our careers at Kentucky. I think we all thought that beating No. 1-ranked Indiana was our championship.

Kevin Grevey

on Kentucky's 1975 Mideast Regional final win
over Indiana to advance to the Final Four

● ● ●

It's such an awesome feeling because some are saying it's the greatest victory in UK basketball ever. They expected it with teams like the Twin Towers and others. I can't describe how I felt when we were up by 20 with 15 minutes to go. The full effect won't sink in until later.

Robert Lock

Wildcat player (1985–88),
on UK's 85–51 blowout of archrival Louisville ,
December 27, 1986

I don't remember very many things that happened. I guess I was just so caught up in all the emotion of the number one and number two teams in the country playing against each other. It was a strange feeling. It was almost like a game I didn't really play in, even though I heard my name mentioned.

Louie Dampier

on his performance in the 1966 NCAA semifinals against No. 2 Duke. Kentucky notched an 83–79 victory behind Dampier's 23 points and 19 from Pat Riley

We were beaten in the first five minutes by a much better team. By the second five minutes, the game was over.

Bobby Knight
*former Indiana head coach,
on the 99–65 shellacking his Hoosiers took
from UK, December 7, 1996*

● ● ●

The harder I tried, the more they wept.

Rick Pitino
*on attempting to console his Wildcats after the
devastating at-the-buzzer 104–103 loss
to Duke in the 1992 East Regional final*

THE SHOT SEEN
'ROUND THE WORLD

It still defies belief.

With just 2.1 seconds remaining in the 1992 NCAA East Regional championship game, with one foot already in the Final Four, Kentuckians held onto their chairs, as Duke's Grant Hill prepared to wing a full-court desperation pass, along with a final prayer, for the Blue Devils.

Seventy-five feet later, the ball came to rest in the artful hands of Duke All-America and Player of the Year Christian Laettner. With milliseconds till the buzzer, Laettner still found time for a fake before propelling a 17-footer toward the basket.

An entire nation collectively gasped as the ball ripped through the ropes. Improbably, Duke had snatched sure victory away from the Wildcats, 104–103. Equally amazing was the fact that The Shot completed a perfect 10-for10 afternoon from the field for Laettner to go along with his 10-for-10 perfection from the charity stripe.

The contest refueled the bitter feelings between the two schools, kicking their rivalry up to a new level of intensity. Laettner's deistic performance was marred only by a technical foul, but a serious one— intentionally stepping on Kentucky freshman Aminu Timberlake.

Kentucky fans will be the first to tell you: They have long memories when it comes to playing Duke.

This time the ending changed. The deep men were covered. The inbounds pass with 4.5 seconds left in the South Region final went short to Duke's William Avery. The freshman guard, whom Kentucky had also recruited, dribbled up the court, getting spun around once on the way, and heaved a running 35-foot shot. And the ball didn't go in. . . . The ending changed. The shot missed. There was no Laettner in the building.

Mark Woods

on the eerie, flashback-type, Christian Laettner-ish ending to the 1998 NCAA South Region final victory over Duke, reminiscent of Kentucky's devastating loss to the Blue Devils in 1992. This time the Wildcats, down by 18 in the first half, won, 86–84, to merit their third consecutive trip to and 13th overall appearance in the Final Four

I don't know if you can call it a rivalry until we win some. I've never beaten Kentucky.

Matt Walsh
Florida forward,
on the Gators' eighth consecutive loss
to Kentucky, 69–66, in Lexington,
on February 8, 2005

● ● ●

Once the game is over, everything that happened prior to that is history.

Tubby Smith
on his Cats' 18th straight SEC victory—
a 69–66 defeat of Florida, UK's eighth win in a
row over the Gators, in early February 2005

THE WILDCAT FAITHFUL

When Pitino took the UK basketball team to Italy in the summer of 1995, a group of Cat fans went along. Of course. One day the group was touring a coliseum in Verona that predated the Roman Colosseum. The tour guide mentioned that the coliseum seated more than 20,000 people. A member of the group murmured, "Hell, our arena's bigger than that."

Pat Forde

I t wasn't until after we had 11,000 fans at our midnight practice, packed houses at our intrasquad scrimmages, 14,000 fans at a morning shooting practice in Louisville, that I realized the impact of the UK program.

Eddie Sutton

◦ ◦ ◦

I didn't think it was to be as much of a goldfish bowl as it was. I had people who would want my autograph because I was Rex Chapman's grandmother. That's carrying it a little bit too far.

Mayme Little Hamby

◦ ◦ ◦

B eing a Kentucky Wildcat fan is the law in our family. . . . If it's blue and white, we're for it.

David Harrod
Frankfort, Kentucky

We have fun; we've got a great bunch of guys; a beautiful program, a super bunch of fans, and when you talk about fans, you talk about those who are with you through thick and thin. There are no other kind.

Joe B. Hall

In 1948, I remember going to New York because [on the way] we made stops in two or three communities in Kentucky. The players went to the rear of the train to the doors and waved. The fans clapped and kind of gave them a send-off on their way to New York [for the NCAA Tournament].

Herky Rupp

I've been coming to the games for about eighteen years. In New Orleans I made national television when I painted a No. 1 on my nose. I still have the tape.

Brooks "Hoot" Gibson
Hazel, Kentucky

❂ ❂ ❂

It's been said ad infinitum that being a basketball fan in Kentucky is a lifelong occupation. Now we know that's incorrect. It's longer than that.

Pat Forde

❂ ❂ ❂

I'm sixty-five years old, and for as long as I can remember I've been a Wildcat fan. Football? No, only roundball for me. Kentucky people just barely know how to spell "football," but we're learning.

Jeanette Lindsey
Paducah, Kentucky

We would get behind, but we wouldn't give up. We never gave up. The fans had a lot to do with it.

Kyle Macy

* * *

I took over a successful program and my job was to keep it successful, and I don't think that was exciting to the fans.

Joe B. Hall

* * *

I've been a Kentucky fan for almost forty years, and I've been listening to Cawood since I was an infant. My family bleeds blue. . . . I've got blue everything—guess you could say I've permanently got the blues.

Monty Hogan
Mandeville, Louisiana

I want the boosters to show me what great fans they are. I want them to give donations to the university, and they can be my friend. But they will stay away from our practices and our players.

Rick Pitino

* * *

No longer is it the days of Pat, Dan, Jimmy Dan, Jack, Kyle, Sam, Rex, and Richie. I'm cheering for Souleymane, Tayshaun, Jamaal, Heshimu, and Nazr. Times are a-changing.

Capt. Dan Armstrong

Cat Chat

* * *

The whole state owns this team.

Rick Pitino

* * *

UK basketball is like a magnet. . . . There are any number of people who live out of state who loyally follow UK.

Dickie Parsons

You, with the blue satin jacket and the face paint and the flag flying from your car.

Pat Forde

* * *

The license plate was bought for me by a friend. I started wearing it around my neck and have really built up a kind of following. People at tournaments come up to me and say, "Hey, Joe," and I don't have any idea who they are. But they remember the license plate. People holler and scream and blow their horn at me. It's kinda neat. I never really thought I'd become a celebrity. I'm just a huge Cats fan.

"Kentucky Joe" Crain
Stanford, Kentucky

I have been to over 1,100 Kentucky basketball games since my first game in the Alumni Gym in 1944. I had attended 615 consecutive games before I had a heart attack and had to miss four games during the Alaska Shootout.

Bill Wiggins
Falmouth, Kentucky

* * *

You find people who have been fans for forty years and have never seen a game, but they listen to the radio and write down everything that happens. You say something, and they will pull the book out and flip through it and tell you whether you are right or wrong.

Ned Jennings
center (1959–61)

We had such a rich UK tradition in our household. I remember when I was 12, home alone with my eight-year-old sister, watching the game on TV while my parents were at the game. I was so fired up, sitting about two feet away from the TV. And then Laettner hit that shot.

Owen Walker

Cincinnati, Ohio

* * *

The people who follow UK live or die basketball. If UK loses a game it's like a death in the family.

Jack Givens

* * *

I don't think you become a Kentucky fan. I think you're born a Kentucky fan.

John Michael Montgomery

*country music artist and Wildcat fan,
Nicholasville, Kentucky*

C ertainly our fans at the University of Kentucky have high expectation levels.

John Pelphrey
*forward (1989–92)/one of Pitino's
Unforgettables*

❋ ❋ ❋

H EY, LOUISVILLE, HOW DO YOU LIKE OUR HAND-ME-DOWNS?

**Sign at the 2001
UK-Louisville game**
*referring to former Wildcat coach Rick Pitino's
return to college coaching in the state of
Kentucky, December 29, 2001, this time as
head man for the Cardinals. The Cats wore
down Louisville, 82–62*

❋ ❋ ❋

T he way the fans have responded leaves me almost speechless. You always have some fans but when I first joined the team I had no idea people would respond like they have.

James Lee
forward (1975–78)

I'd just as soon freeze to death.

Ashley Judd

actress and UK graduate,
on being offered a University of
North Carolina jacket on a chilly movie set

* * *

The acceptance and response I've had from the fans since I've been here has been overwhelming. Fans identify with Kentucky basketball more so than they do with anything else because of the great tradition, which is something that goes all the way back, even before Adolph Rupp.

Tubby Smith

* * *

When you see Kentucky's fans, you just wonder. You think how wonderful it would be to go to their school. You wish you could trade places for a day, just so you could experience that feeling.

Kris Johnson
former UCLA player

When I came out of high school, I had over nine-hundred scholarship offers, and the fans were the reason why I opted to come to the University of Kentucky. They always said basketball was a way of life in the Bluegrass State. Not until I was here did I realize just how important it really is.

Sam Bowie

✿ ✿ ✿

I'm thinking about getting a permanent blue streak in my hair.

La Donna Walters
Campbellsville, Kentucky

I became a true fan at the age of ten. All my uncles would sit around and listen to Kentucky basketball on the radio, and if you couldn't be quiet, then you couldn't be in the room while the game was on. So at the age of ten I got to where I could be quiet enough, and that's when I started listening to Cawood. I've stayed with it ever since. It's a religion in Kentucky, being a fan of the Wildcats. The whole state is like a family.

Greg Mays
Burlington, Kentucky

B eing a Wildcat fan is a genetic thing. If you're born in the state of Kentucky, you're a fan.

Eddie Montgomery
of the country music duo Montgomery Gentry,
Lexington, Kentucky

I became a fan before I was able to talk.

Gene Courtney
Florence, Kentucky

THE
BALL BAG

As a kid, I'd listen to Kentucky on the radio at the kitchen table, and I'd keep score myself. I remember reading that Wah Jones drank milk every day. That really impressed me. I love Kentucky basketball.

Joe B. Hall

Bob McAdoo told me that when Kentucky got beat by Texas Western [1966 NCAA championship game] it was more than just a basketball game. He and other black players said that game meant the difference to their being able to feel comfortable about starting to go to predominantly white schools in the South.

Pat Riley

● ● ●

They can run a hell of a lot faster and jump a hell of a lot higher. Some of those kids can jump up and sit on the basket. None of us could, that's for sure.

Cliff Barker

*forward (1947–49) and member of
the Fabulous Five,
comparing today's athletes with the players
of the late 1940s*

Somebody asked me a little while back if Pat was always a flashy dresser and I said, Yeah, he was always a modern dresser. They asked because of the way he dresses now, always in the best of clothes. He was that way. He stayed up with the best of styles and whatever was in style he tried to get that for himself.

Louie Dampier

*on the sartorial splendor of teammate
and later legendary NBA coach Pat Riley*

* * *

If that's what he got, he's smarter than the fella that gave it to him.

Adolph Rupp

*on LSU superstar Pete Maravich's rumored
$1 million pro deal*

He doesn't need to look at the tape. He's got a scoreboard hanging over his head, for heaven's sake.

Charlie Spoonhour

*former Saint Louis University head coach,
on Tubby Smith's post-game comment to reporters
that he'd have to view the videotape of UK's
dominating 88–61 victory of Spoonhour's
Billikens in 1998 to see how well his Wildcats
played. Kentucky advanced to the NCAA's
Sweet Sixteen with the win*

No, I like my bulls to enjoy their work.

Adolph Rupp

*when asked if he artificially inseminated
the cattle he owned*

Cliff Barker broke his nose and the [AAU champion] Phillips Oilers beat us, 53–49. The winning team provided the head Olympic coach. The losing team, which was us, provided the assistant. The first thing [Adolph Rupp] said to us was, "I want to thank you sons of bitches for making me an assistant coach for the first time in my career."

Ralph Beard

on the oddities of selecting the 1948 U.S. Olympic Basketball Team and coaches

When I met the pope, I leaned over and kissed his ring. Then he looked at my hand to do the same, and he said, "Oh, you don't have a ring."

Rick Pitino

returning from a trip to Italy in the summer of 1995

oach Rupp came up like a dog on a point, and he said, "Harry, who in the hell is doing that whistling out there?" Says, "By God, if he wants to sing, we'll send him over to the music Guignol [the student fine-arts theater]. Out here we play basketball."

Ralph Beard

on Wildcat Jim Line, who had the temerity to whistle during a Kentucky shooting drill in the late 1940s. Rupp's rhetorical question was asked of assistant coach Harry Lancaster, who was supervising the shoot-around

TWO-SPORT ATHLETES:
A WILDCAT TRADITION

Kentucky has fashioned its share of remarkable all-around athletes down through the decades.

In the late 19th and early 20th century, it was not uncommon for the University's better athletes to compete in a number of sports. But it became more and more of a rarity as skill and proficiency in athletics increased.

In addition, sports were becoming big business. The age of specialization required an athlete to make a choice and play his favorite or best sport. The following are some of the Kentucky basketball stars who resisted one-sport concentration to excel in two (or more):

Frank Ramsey, C. M. Newton, Cotton Nash, Dick Parsons, Randy Embry, Allen Feldhaus are just some of the Wildcats who dug substantial marks in the diamond dust of Hagan Stadium while at Kentucky. Joe "Red" Hagan, who once held the record for the longest basket made by a Wildcat, played end and was captain of the 1937 Kentucky football team.

Without rival is three-sport star Wallace "Wah Wah" Jones, a member of the hallowed Fabulous Five and a second-team consensus All-America forward in 1949. Jones also starred as a two-time All-SEC end for Bear Bryant in football and was a pitching standout for the Wildcats in baseball. In all, he garnered 11 UK letters.

WAH WAH PEDAL
TO THE METAL

The aforementioned Wah Wah Jones's all-around athletic ability once caught the eye of Chicago Bears head coach George Halas, arguably the most important figure in pro football history. "I was offered $8,500 to play with the Chicago Bears," Jones once recalled. "I guess you always wonder how you would have come out."

Kentucky teammate and future Pro Football Hall of Fame legend George Blanda, who threw more than one pass Wah Wah's way while both starred for Kentucky, was offered $7,500 to play for Halas.

"He stayed with the Bears and I came back to Indianapolis," said Jones.

As a part owner and star member of the NBA Indianapolis Olympians, along with the other members of Kentucky's once-Fabulous Five, the decision to remain in basketball appeared to be the right call for Jones. But then came the scandal. One year later, unable to draw crowds without their two biggest stars, Beard and Groza, the NBA team broke up.

I'd put the center-jump back in and take off the backboards and net. Just leave the hoop. And raise the hoop five feet.

Adolph Rupp
to a New York writer,
on how to improve the game

* * *

You may think it's your time as a senior to play and then the coach goes out and recruits a bunch of good players and you just drop a little farther behind. It's a big business. You have to grow up and face the facts that your career has to end some-time . . . and then you have to move on to something else. That's the whole thing about getting an education, so you can be prepared when it does end.

G. J. Smith
Wildcat player (1973–75)

PARALLEL MARKED
1966 SEASON
FOR CATS, MINERS

An interesting equivalent linked the foes of the landmark 1966 NCAA finals. Both Kentucky and Texas Western were undefeated, having won 23 straight before losing their first games of the season, on the same night, just two weeks before the start of the NCAA Tournament.

● ● ●

¿CÓMO ESTÁ USTED?

In the late 1940s, on a road trip to New York City, several Wildcat stars, including Wah Wah Jones and Kenny Rollins of the Fabulous Five, took in singer Perry Como's show at Radio City Music Hall. When the players returned to the hotel, they ran into Coach Rupp, who inquired where the boys had been.

"We've been to see Perry Como," said one of the Wildcats.

Rupp questioned further. "Who does he play for?"

How big a wad of gum do I chew during a game? Oh, I'd say a hunk of five cakes. . . . Yes, sir, I chew even when I ain't playing . . . that is, except when I'm asleep or eating. . . . No, sir, I don't prefer any particular brand. . . . You say that costs me about $36.50 a year? . . . Oh no, sir! A drugstore in Lexington gives me all my gum for nothing. They give it to me in cartons.

Ralph Beard
1948

They ought to go back and give me a point for every field goal I made because all of mine were from the three-point range.

Wah Wah Jones
*on the three-point line, nonexistent during
Jones's playing days (1946–49)*

That was no zone. That was a stratified transitional hyperbolic paraboloid with a man between the ball and the basket.

Adolph Rupp

● ● ●

Spike Lee and Muhammad Ali each sat on the UK bench for games. Actress Ashley Judd tried to sit. Couldn't keep still. Kept squirming, getting up on her knees, waving pom-poms as her beloved Cats rallied from a 22-point deficit at Vanderbilt's quirky old Memorial Gymnasium.

Mark Woods

● ● ●

The legislature should pass a law that at three o'clock every afternoon, any basketball coach who is 70 years old gets a shot of bourbon. These damned bouncing, bouncing, bouncing basketballs are putting me to sleep.

Adolph Rupp

in 1972, his last year as coach of Kentucky

When they called and said they were going to retire his jersey, I wondered what they were going to retire, because he never played for Kentucky. I was curious. I thought, maybe, they would have something that looked like a brown suit coat up there.

Herky Rupp
*on his father Adolph Rupp's retired jersey,
hanging in the rafters of Rupp Arena*

⚾ ⚾ ⚾

Kentucky will always be in my heart.

Rick Pitino

⚾ ⚾ ⚾

This is it, fellows. Forty minutes to glory.

Joe B. Hall
*to his players before taking the court for the
1978 NCAA championship game vs. Duke*

Basketball.

Joe B. Hall
*when asked during the 1975 NCAA Tournament
what the B in his middle name stood for*

KENTUCKY
NATIONAL CHAMPION
ROSTERS

*I*n the seven national championship seasons in Lexington, many a Wildcat has played the cog in the wheel. The following roster listings are a salute to all the players that have helped spell National Champions for Kentucky.

1947–48
36–3
World champions (Olympic gold medal),
NCAA national champions
Adolph Rupp, coach

	Pos.	Hgt.	Wt.	Class
Clifford Barker	F	6–2	185	Jr
Dale Barnstable	F	6–3	175	So
Ralph Beard	G	5–10	175	Jr
Albert Campbell	C	6–4	200	Sr
Albert Cummins	G	5–10	160	So
Alex Groza	C	6–7	220	Jr
Robert Henne	F	6–1	165	Fr
Walter Hirsch	F	6–3	180	Fr
Joseph Holland	F	6–4	190	Jr
Wallace Jones	F	6–4	205	Jr
James Jordan	F	6–3	185	So
James Line	F	6–2	185	So
Jack Parkinson	G	6–0	175	Sr
Kenneth Rollins	G	6–0	175	Sr
Will Smether	G	6–2	180	Fr
John Stough	G	6–0	170	So
Garland Townes	G	6–0	170	Fr

Starters in bold

1948–49
32–2
NCAA national champions
Adolph Rupp, coach

	Pos.	Ht.	Wt.	Class
Clifford Barker	F	6–2	185	Sr
Dale Barnstable	G	6–3	180	Jr
Ralph Beard	G	5–10	176	Sr
Roger Day	F	6–3	185	So
Alex Groza	C	6–7	220	Sr
Joe Hall	G	6–0	165	So
Bob Henne	G	6–1	170	So
Walter Hirsch	C-F	6–4	185	So
Wallace Jones	C-F	6–4	205	Sr
James Line	F	6–2	190	Jr
Johnny Stough	G	6–0	170	Jr
Garland Townes	G	6–0	180	So

1950–51
32–2
NCAA national champions
Adolph Rupp, coach

	Pos.	Ht.	Wt.	Class
Lindle Castle	G	5–11	165	So
*Cliff Hagan	C-F	6–4	210	Fr
Walt Hirsch (Capt.)	F-C	6–3	185	Sr
Paul Lansaw	F	6–2	180	Jr
Roger Layne	C	6–7	185	Sr
Shelby Linville	F-C	6–5	210	Jr
Read Morgan	F	6–4	200	Jr
C. M. Newton	G-F	6–2	190	Jr
Dwight Price	F	6–2	175	So
Frank Ramsey	G-F	6–3	180	So
Bill Spivey	C	7–0	215	Jr
Guy Strong	G	6–0	165	Jr
Louis Tsioropoulos	C-F	6–5	195	So
Bobby Watson	G	5–10	175	Jr
Lucian Whitaker	G	6–0	175	Jr

*Not eligible until end of first semester, January 26, 1951

1957–58
23–6
NCAA national champions
Adolph Rupp, coach

	Pos.	Ht.	Wt.	Class
Earl Adkins	G	6–4	180	Sr
Ed Beck	C	6–7	188	Sr
Bill Cassady	F-G	6–2	191	Sr
Lincoln Collinsworth	G	6–3	185	Sr
E.A. Couch	G	6–0	180	So
Johnny Cox	F	6–4	185	Jr
John Crigler	F-G	6–3	180	Sr
Vernon Hatton	G	6–3	188	Sr
Dick Howe	C-F	6–5	208	Jr
Lowell Hughes	G	6–0	175	So
Phil Johnson	F-C	6–6	190	Jr
Don Mills	C	6–7	190	So
Harold Ross	G	6–2	180	Sr
Bill Smith	F	6–5	203	Sr
Adrian Smith	G	6–0	178	Sr

1977–78
30–2
NCAA national champions
Joe B. Hall, coach

	Pos.	Ht.	Wt.	Class
Chuck Aleksinas	C	6–10	250	Fr
Dwane Casey	G	6–2	195	Jr
Truman Claytor	G	6–1	178	Jr
Scott Courts	C-F	6–10	230	Fr
Fred Cowan	F	6–8	195	Fr
Chris Gettelfinger	G	6–2	185	Fr
Jack Givens	F	6–4	205	Sr
James Lee	F	6–5	230	Sr
Kyle Macy	G	6–3	180	So
Mike Phillips	C	6–10	240	Sr
Rick Robey	F-C	6–10	230	Sr
Jay Shidler	G	6–1	185	So
Tim Stephens	G	6–3	180	So
LaVon Williams	F	6–6	205	So

1995–96
34–2
NCAA national champions
Rick Pitino, coach

	Pos	Ht.	Wt.	Class
Tony Delk	G	6–1	195	Sr
Allen Edwards	G	6–5	195	So
Wayne Turner	G	6–2	180	Fr
Nazr Mohammed	C	6–10	230	Fr
Jeff Sheppard	G	6–3	185	Jr
Cameron Mills	G	6–3	180	So
Derek Anderson	F-G	6–5	180	Jr
Antoine Walker	F	6–8	220	So
Anthony Epps	G	6–2	185	Jr
Ron Mercer	G-F	6–7	220	Fr
Walter McCarty	F-C	6–10	230	Sr
Mark Pope	C	6–10	240	Sr
Oliver Simmons	F	6–8	210	Fr

1997–1998
35–4
NCAA national champions
Tubby Smith, coach

	Pos.	Ht.	Wt.	Class
Myron Anthony	F	6–7	220	Fr
Michael Bradley	F-C	6–10	230	Fr
Allen Edwards	G-F	6–5	200	Sr
Heshimu Evans	F	6–6	210	Jr
Ryan Hogan	G	6–3	193	Fr
Jamaal Magloire	C	6–10	240	So
Steve Masiello	G	6–2	175	So
Cameron Mills	G	6–3	190	Sr
Nazr Mohammed	C	6–10	240	Jr
Scott Padgett	F	6–9	229	Jr
Jeff Sheppard	G	6–3	190	Sr
Saul Smith	G	6–2	170	Fr
Wayne Turner	G	6–2	187	Jr

BIBLIOGRAPHY

Baron, Randall S. and Russell Rice. *The Official University of Kentucky Basketball Book.* Louisville, Ky.: Devyn Press, Inc., 1986.

Bergeron, Elena. "Guard Dogs: Trespass on their turf and they will bite back." *ESPN the Magazine,* March 28, 2005: 76.

Bradley, Michael. *The Sporting News presents Big Blue: 100 Years of Kentucky Wildcats Basketball.* St. Louis, Mo.: The Sporting News, 2002.

Bozich, Rick and Pat Forde, C. Ray Hall and Mark Woods. *A Legacy of Champions.* Indianapolis, Ind.: Masters Press, 1997.

Bynum, Mike, ed. *Comeback Cats: The 1997–98 Kentucky Wildcats' Unforgettable National Championship Sea-* son. Louisville, Ky.: Courier-Journal, 1998.

Davis, Brad, ed. 1985–86 *University of Kentucky Basketball Facts Book.* Lexington, Ky.: Host Communications, 1985.

Davis, Brad, ed. 1987–88 *University of Kentucky Basketball Facts Book.* Lexington, Ky.: Host Communications, 1987.

Downing, Brooks. *1998–99 Kentucky Basketball Media Guide.* Lexington, Ky.: University of Kentucky Athletics Association, 1998.

Embry, Mike. *Basketball in the Bluegrass State: The Championship Teams.* New York: Leisure Press, 1983.

Fitzgerald, Francis J. *The Legacy & The Glory.* Louisville, Ky.: AdCraft Sports Marketing, 1995.

Kaneshiro, Stacey. "Padgett, Kentucky Escape 92–88 in OT." *USA TODAY*, 15 March 1999: 4C.

Kindred, Dave. *Basketball—The Dream Game in Kentucky.* Louisville, Ky.: Data Courier, Inc., 1976.

Kuhn, Ken, ed. *University of Kentucky 1949 Basketball Facts.* Lexington, Ky.: UK Dept. of Public Relations, 1949.

Kuhn, Ken, ed. *University of Kentucky 1967–68 Basketball Facts.* Lexington, Ky.: UK Dept. of Public Relations, 1967.

Laudeman, Tev. *The Rupp Years.* Louisville, Ky.: The Courier-Journal, The Louisville Times, 1972.

Ledford, Cawood. *Heart of Blue.* Lexington, Ky.: Host Communications, Inc., 1995.

Ledford, Cawood. *Six Roads to Glory.* Lexington, Ky.: Host Communications, Inc., 1997.

McGill, John and Walt Johnson. *A Year at the Top: Kentucky Wildcats '77-'78.* Lexington, Ky.: Jim Host and Associates Inc., 1978.

McLean, Terri Darr and Gene Abell, eds. *Bravo Blue! Relive Kentucky's Memorable 1995–96 Season.* Lexington, Ky.: Lexington Herald-Leader Company, 1996.

Nelli, Bert and Steve Nelli.

The Winning Tradition: A History of Kentucky Wildcat Basketball, Second Edition. Lexington, Ky.: The University Press of Kentucky, 1998.

Newton, C. M. as told to Billy Reed. *Newton's Laws: The C. M. Newton Story.* Lexington, Ky.: Host Communications, Inc., 2000.

Parks, Shannon. *Catmania.* Chicago: Triumph Books, 1999.

Polley, Mandy and Scott Stricklin. *2004–05 Kentucky Basketball Media Guide.* Lexington, Ky.: University of Kentucky Athletics Department, 2004.

Quimby, John M. *Fab Fifty: A Kentucky Wildcat Fan Over Fifty Years.* Schenectady, N.Y.: Duffield & Moore Books, 1999.

Rice, Russell. *Kentucky Basketball's Big Blue Machine.* Huntsville, Ala.: The Strode Publishers, 1978.

Rice, Russell. *Kentucky's Basketball Baron.* Champaign, Ill.: Sagamore Publishing, 1994.

Stacy, Randy and Russell Rice. *Official Kentucky Basketball 1983–84.*

Thurman, Tom, ed. *Hardwood Heaven: Basketball in Kentucky, 1895–1966.* Louisville, Ky.: Butler Book Publishing Services, 2003.

Trease, Denny. *Tales from the*

Kentucky Hardwood: A Collection of the Greatest Kentucky Basketball Stories Ever Told! Sports Publishing LLC, 2002.

Vaught, Jamie H. *Cats Up Close: Champions of Kentucky Basketball.* Kuttawa, Ky.: McClanahan Publishing House, 1999.

Vaught, Jamie H. *Crazy About the Cats.* Kuttawa, Ky.: McClanahan Publishing House, 1992.

Vaught, Jamie H. Still *Crazy About the Cats.* Kuttawa, Ky.: McClanahan Publishing House, 1996.

Wallace, Tom. *Kentucky Basketball Encyclopedia.* Champaign, Ill.: Sports Publishing LLC, 2001.

Wheeler, Lonnie. *Blue Yonder.* Wilmington, Ohio: Orange Frazer Press, 1998.

● ● ●

WEBSITES:

Associated Press. "Kentucky Makes 13 of 19 3-pointers." sports.espn.go.com/ncb/recap?gameId=250570333, Feb. 26, 2005.

Associated Press. "Wildcats rally past Gators again." sports.espn.go.com/ncb/recap?gameId=250390096, Feb. 8, 2005.

Associated Press. "Wildcats only undefeated team in conference." Jan. 25, 2005

ESPN.com news services. "Spartans rebound from desperate 3, seize control in second OT." sports-att.espn.go.com/ncb/recap?gameId=254000046, March 27, 2005

Forde, Pat. "Rondo, Cats scratch Gators (again)." ESPN.com. http://proxy.espn.go.com/ncb/columns/story?columnist=forde_pat&id=1987436, Feb. 8, 2005.

Forde, Pat. ESPN.com. sports.espn.go.com/ncb/ncaatourney05/news/story?id=2023367, March 27, 2005.

Lexington Herald Leader, www.ukfans.net/jps/uk/wildcats.html, Aug. 15,1996.

Wieberg, Steve. "Spartans 2OT win puts capper on wild regionals." *USA TODAY.* www.usatoday.com/sports/college/mensbasketball/tourney05/2005–03–27-overtimes_x.htm, March 28, 2005.

INDEX

A
Abell, Gene, 246
Adkins, Earl, 241
Air Pair, 84
Alabama Crimson Tide, 20, 42, 52, 150
Alamodome, 149
Alaska Shootout, 216
Aleksinas, Chuck, 242
Ali, Muhammad, 234
Allen, Forrest C. "Phog," 16, 93
Alumni Gym, 131, 181-185, 216
Amateur Athletic Union (AAU), 56, 130, 227
American Basketball Association, 158
American Hereford Journal, 95
Anderson, Derek, 41, 43, 84, 243
Anderson, Dwight, 142
Anthony, Myron, 244
Archibald, Nate, 72
Arkansas Razorbacks, 23, 145
Armstrong, Dan, 214
Ashford, Ed, 189
Assembly Hall, 108
Associated Press, 59, 164
Auerbach, Red, 63
Avenue of Champions, 183
Avery, William, 207

B
Barker, Clifford, 29, 32-33, 132, 153, 165-166, 224, 227, 238-239
Barker Hall, 181-182
Barnstable, Dale, 115, 117-119, 238-239
Basketball Hall of Fame, 154, 159
Baylor, Elgin, 128
Beard, Frank, 58
Beard, Ralph, 6, 29, 33-34, 51, 53, 55-56, 57, 59, 89, 115-117, 120-121, 130, 132, 153, 157, 159-160, 165-166, 169, 190-191, 227-228, 230, 233, 238-239
Beard, Sue, 56
Bearup, Bret, 19, 48, 111
Beck, Ed, 89, 241
Bee, Clair, 53
Bennett, Winston, 38
Berger, Cliff, 36
Blanda, George, 230
Boeck, Larry, 133, 166, 170, 195
Bogans, Keith, 43
Bounds, Brad, 36
Bowie, Sam, 13, 39, 106, 192, 220
Bozich, Rick, 51, 108-109, 146, 198
Bradley, Michael, 38, 40-43, 59, 65, 78, 83, 85-86, 156, 158, 178, 184, 186, 188, 244

Brassow, Jeff, 145
Brown, Dale, 124, 143
Brown, Hubie, 72
Browning, Bud, 56
Bryant, Paul "Bear," 20, 59, 94, 108, 229
Buchheit, George, 182
Buell Armory, 181
Burr, Jim, 152
Burrow, Bob, 153, 185

C
Campbell, Albert, 238
Carey, Burgess, 14
Casey, Dwane, 40, 107, 123, 125, 242
Cassady, Bill, 241
Castle, Lindle, 240
Chandler, Happy, 13, 132
Chapman, Rex, 22, 79-81, 143, 210, 214
Chapman, Wayne, 22
Checkerdome, 140
Chicago Bears, 230
Cincinnati Bearcats, 28
Claytor, Truman, 242
Clevenger, Steve, 36
Collinsworth, Lincoln, 241
Columbia University, 95
Combs, Oscar, 47
Como, Perry, 232
Conley, Larry, 29, 36, 195
Conner, Jimmy Dan, 37, 79, 173, 185
Coomes, Mark, 12, 25,

146, 166
Couch, E. A., 241
Courtney, Gene, 222
Courts, Scott, 242
Cousy, Bob, 157
Cowan, Fred, 242
Cox, Johnny, 161, *162*, 185, 241
Crain, "Kentucky Joe" 215
Cremins, Bobby, 111
Crigler, John, 241
Crook, Herbert, 80
Cummins, Albert, 238
Curci, Fran, 47

D
Daley, Arthur, 163
Dampier, Louie, 49, 71-72, *73*, 92, 99, 136, 153, 158, 160-161, 185-186, 204, 225
Darr, Terri, 246
Davender, Ed, 40, 80
Day, Roger, 239
Dayton Arena, 138
Dean, Joe Jr., 107
DeCourcy, Mike, 112
Dee, Johnny, 103
Deford, Frank, 69, 88, 90
Delk, Tony, 43, 197, 243
DeMoisey, Frenchy, 29-30
Dinwiddie, Jim, 89
Donovan, Herman, 132
Duke Blue Devils, 42, 67, 107, 139-141, 144, 147, 197, 199, 201-202, 204-207, 235

E
Edwards, Allen, 243-244
Edwards, LeRoy, 29-32
Effrat, Louis, 190
Elite Eight, 23
Embry, Randy, 229
Emery Air Freight (Emery Worldwide), 123, 125
Epps, Anthony, 243
ESPN, 13, 43, 151
Evans, Billy, 153
Evans, Heshimu, 244

F
Fabulous Five, 16, 29, 32, 34, 62, 115-117, 130,

132, 134, 164-169, 176, 183, 224, 229, 232
Farmer, Richie, 26, 29, 202
Feldhaus, Allen, 229
Feldhaus, Deron, 26, 40
Fiddlin' Five, 17, 134, 170, 180
Flash, Pat, 70
Florida Gators, 208
Forbes magazine, 95
Ford, Travis, 41
Forde, Pat, 13, 44, 149, 151, 177, 209, 212, 215
Forrest C. "Phog" Allen, 16
Frazier, Walt, 72
Freedom Hall, 134, 143, 187

G
Gamble, Gary, 36
Georgetown Hoyas, 111
Georgia Bulldogs, 28, 103, 111, 133, 189
Georgia Tech Yellow Jackets, 111, 189
Gettelfinger, Chris, 242
Gibson, Brooks "Hoot," 212
Givens, Jack "Goose," 22, 77, 139-140, 185, 217, 242
Gminski, Mike, 140
Gomelsky, Alexander, 175
Goodrich, Gail, 140
Grawemeyer, Phil, 65
Grevey, Kevin, 29, 37, 160, 202-203
Groza, Alex, 29, 34, 59, *60*, 62, 96, 100, 115, 160, 165-166, 169, 230, 238-239
Guignol, 228

H
Hagan, Cliff, 29, *64*, 65-66, 90, 135, 153-154, 160, 185, 240
Hagan, Joe "Red," 132
Hagan Stadium, 229
Halas, George, 230
Hall, C. Ray, 49, 87-88, 90, 93, 102-103, 110, 171-172, 182, 245
Hall, Joe B., 13, 19-21, 23-24, 33, 38, 45, 47, 51, 55,

71, 76-79, 100, 102, 106-109, 114, 127, 131, 138, 140-142, 164, 173-174, 191, 198, 211, 213, 223, 235-236, 242
Hamby, Mayme Little, 210
Hammond, Tom, 113
Harden, Roger, 29, 39
Harrod, David, 210
Hatton, Vernon, 66, 98, 128-129, 134, 241
Hayden, Basil, 14, 181
Hayes, Chuck, 49-50, 150
Hedric, Darrell, 174
Heifetz, Jascha, 170
Helms Foundation, 30-31, 61
Henne, Robert "Bob," 238-239
Heyman, Art, 67
Hill, Grant, 144, 199, 206
Hirsch, Walter, 238-240
Hobbs, David, 42
Hogan, Monty, 213
Hogan, Ryan, 244
Holland, Joseph, 238
Host, Jim, 246
Houston Cougars, 39
Howe, Dick, 241
HSBI Report, 83
Hughes, Lowell, 241

I
Indiana Hoosiers, 69, 78, 108, 138, 202-203, 205
Indianapolis Olympians, 169, 230
Issel, Dan, 29, 32, 74, *75*, 76, 82, 92, 96, 114, 137, 153, 156, 160, 185, 193

J
Jennings, Ned, 216
Johnson, Kris, 219
Johnson, Phil, 241
Johnson, Magic, 84
Jones, Wallace "Wah Wah," 34, *35*, 94, 129, 153, 161, 165-166, 192, 223, 229-230, 232-233, 238-239
Jordan, James, 238
Jucker, Ed, 28
Judd, Ashley, 219, 234

K

Kansas Jayhawks, 16, 93, 142, 196
Kansas State Wildcats, 133
Kentucky Colonels, 158
Kindred, Dave, 15, 33, 55-56, 58, 61, 63, 65, 74, 89, 93, 153, 157, 190, 246
King, Bernard, 82
King High School, 83
Kirkpatrick, Curry, 143
Knight, Bob, 78, 108, 11-112, 205
Konchalski, Tom, 83
Kron, Tommy, 29, 36, 50
Krzyzewski, Mike, 111
Kurland, Bob, 130

L

Laettner, Christian, 144, 199, 206-207, 217
Lancaster, Harry, 55, 66, 70, 74, 102, 104, 167-169, 228
Lansaw, Paul, 240
Lapchick, Joe, 164
Laudeman, Tev, 34, 54, 63, 154
Lawrence, David, 30
Layne, Roger, 240
Ledford, Cawood, 24, 37, 77, 79, 110, 112, 136, 170, 213, 221
Lee, James, 38, 78, 218, 242
Lee, Spike, 234
LeMaster, Jim, 36
Lentz, Larry, 36
Lewis, Guy, 39
Lexington Center, 20, 187
Lexington Herald, 189
Lincoln, Abraham, 97
Lindsey, Jeanette, 212
Lindsey, Robert, 27
Line, James "Jim," 228, 238-239
Linville, Shelby, 240
Lock, Robert, 203
Lombardi, Vincent, 108
Los Angeles Lakers, 70
Louisville Cardinals, 143, 180, 218
Louisville Courier-Journal, 12-13, 15, 25, 27, 49, 51,

80, 133, 146, 166, 171, 176, 189, 195
Loyola Ramblers, 195
LSU Tigers, 25, 75, 124, 143, 145-146, 196, 225
Lyons, Ronnie, 153

M

Macy, Kyle, 45, 78, 142, 160-161, 213, 242
Madison Square Garden, 117, 130, 164, 190
Magloire, Jamaal, 42, 244
Malone, Karl, 82
Maravich, Pete, 75, 225
Marquette Warriors (Golden Eagles), 11, 132
Mashburn, Jamal, 21, 29, 82-83, 155, 160
Masiello, Steve, 244
Mays, Greg, 221
McAdoo, Bob, 224
McBrayer, Paul, 30
McCarty, Walter, 243
McDonald, Jim, 153
McGill, Ralph, 163
McGuire, Al, 11-12, 18, 24, 27, 188
McHale, Kevin, 82
Memorial Coliseum, 138, 175, 184-187, 189
Memorial Gymnasium, 234
Mercer, Ron, 29, 43, 84-85, 243
Miami Heat, 70
Miami (Ohio) RedHawks, 174
Michigan State Spartans, 50, 151-152, 200
Mikan, George, 61, 135
Mills, Cameron, 112, 180, 243-244
Mills, Chris, 23, 123
Mills, Claude, 123
Mills, Don, 241
Mills, Terry, 98
Minneapolis Lakers, 135
Minniefield, Dirk, 38
Mississippi State Bulldogs, 138, 163
Mohammed, Nazr, 243-244
Montgomery, Eddie, 222
Montgomery, John Michael, 217

Montgomery Gentry, 222
Moran, Malcolm, 144
Morgan, Read, 240
Moss, Ravi, 52
Mullins, Jeff, 67

N

Naismith, James A., 16, 144
Nash, Cotton, 9, 67-69, 153, 160-161, 185, 229
National Basketball Assn. (NBA), 22, 25, 70, 82, 120, 135, 157, 161, 169, 196, 202, 225, 230
National Invitation Tournament (NIT), 15-16, 34, 159, 166, 190, 195
NCAA Austin Regional, 50, 151-152
NCAA championship game, 17, 70, 133, 139, 147, 172, 194-195, 224, 235
NCAA East Regional, 144, 146, 199, 202, 205-206
NCAA Final Four, 36, 43, 77, 100, 108, 128, 138, 158, 174, 177, 197, 199, 203, 206-207
NCAA Finals, 107, 140, 173, 175, 197, 232
NCAA Mideast Regional, 108, 138, 202-203
NCAA Midwest Regional, 196
NCAA South Regional, 42, 147, 197, 207
NCAA Sweet Sixteen, 226
NCAA Tournament, 28, 48, 86, 128, 148, 150, 200, 211, 232, 236
NCAA West Regional, 85
Nelli, Bert, 31, 61-62, 104, 167, 179, 200, 246
Nelli, Steve, 31, 61-62, 104, 167, 179, 200, 246
New York Giants, 199
New York Times, 144, 163, 190
Newton, C. M., 110, 121-122, 147, 195, 229, 240
North Carolina Tar Heels, 67, 111-112, 219
NYU Violets, 15

O

Oakley, Charles, 82
Ohio State Buckeyes, 41
Oklahoma A&M Aggies, 130
Olajuwon, Akeem, 39
Ole Miss Rebels, 103, 137, 180
Oliva, Bob, 83
Olympic Fund, 130
Olympic Games, 15, 34, 129, 167
Osborn, Eric, 123

P

Padgett, Scott, 178, 196, 244
Palmer, Arnold, 58
Parkinson, Jack, 238
Parsons, Dickie, 99, 103, 159, 214, 229
Payne, Tom, 20
Pelphrey, John, 26, 218
Perkins, Ray, 20
Phillips, Mike, 78, 242
Phillips Oilers, 227
Phillips 66ers, 56, 130
Pitino, Rick, 18, 21-22, 25-26, 28, 40-41, 46-48, 50, 82-85, 109-113, 126, 145, 155, 160, 175, 190, 196, 200-201, 205, 209, 214, 218, 227, 235, 243
Pitino's Bombinos, 26
Pope, Mark, 243
Porter, Tommy, 36
Poteet, Yogi, 67
Pratt, Mike, 32
Price, Dwight, 240
Prince, Tayshaun, 86, 150, 214
Pro Football Hall of Fame, 230
Professional Golfers' Assn. (PGA), 58
Pursiful, Larry, 36, 67, 153

Q

Quimby, John M., 74

R

Radio City Music Hall, 232
Ramsey, Frank, 46, 63, 153, 160-161, 185, 229, 240

Reed, Billy, 24, 27, 120, 246
Rice, Russell, 32, 59, 97, 164-165
Riley, Pat, 32, 36, 49, 69-71, 84, 111, 172, 185, 193, 204, 224-225
Robey, Rick, 78, 242
Rolling Stones, 147
Rollins, Kenneth "Kenny," 29, 33, 132, 153, 165-166, 168-169, 232, 238
Rondo, Rajon, 43-44
Rose, Gayle, 135
Ross, Harold, 241
Rupp, Adolph Frederick "Baron of the Bluegrass," 9, 13-14, 16, 20, 23-24, 27, 29-32, 46, 48, 53, 55, 62-63, 66, 71, 87-90, *91*, *101*, 103, 108, 114, 116, 119, 121, 130-132, 134, 138, 140, 153, 157, 159-160, *162*, 171, 173, 176, 184, 186-187, 191-195, 197, 200, 219, 225-228, 231-235, 238-241
Rupp, Herky, 94, 105, 211, 235
Rupp Arena, 21-22, 184, 186-188, 235
Rupp's Runts, 17, 29, 36, 70, 171, 180, 194-195
Ruth, Babe, 58

S

Saint Louis Billikens, 226
Seattle Chieftains, 134
SEC Tournament, 16, 23, 28, 42, 52, 145, 163
Sewanee Tigers, 20
Sheppard, Jeff, 43, 177, 197, 243-244
Shidler, Jay, 242
Shot, The, 30, 36, 65, 72, 128-129, 132, 139, 151, 158, 199, 206-207
Simmons, Oliver, 243
Sinatra, Frank, 147
Slaughterhouse Five, 173
Smether, Will, 238
Smith, Adrian, 241
Smith, Bill, 241
Smith, Dean, 111-112
Smith, G. J., 90, 231

Smith, Saul, 244
Smith, Orlando "Tubby," 28, 43, 49, 52, 112-113, 148, 176, 179-180, 200, 208, 219, 226, 244
Southeastern Conference (SEC), 15-17, 23, 28, 36, 42, 52, 76, 81, 85, 115, 137, 140, 145-146, 150, 159, 163, 176, 208
Southern Intercollegiate Conference, 181
Soviet National Team, 175
Spanarkle, Jim, 139
Sparks, Patrick, 150-152
Spicer, Carey, 14, 29
Spielberg, Steven, 146
Spivey, Bill, 61, 115, 120, 122, 133, 185, 240
Spoonhour, Charlie, 226
SPORT magazine, 9, 19, 69, 130, 166, 191, 229
Sporting News, 245
Sports Illustrated, 23, 69, 82, 88, 123, 126, 143
Stallcup, Mac, 142
Steele, Larry, 29
Stephens, Tim, 242
Stewart, Gene, 36
Stoll Field, 130
Stough, John "Johnny," 238-239
Streit, Saul S., 119
Strong, Guy, 240
Sutton, Eddie, 12, 23, 26, 46-47, 81, 93, 109, 112, 124, 191, 210
Sweet, Ozzie, 9
Syracuse Orange, 77, 175, 197

T

Tallent, Bob, 36
Temple Owls, 128-129
Tennessee Volunteers, 3, 49, 132
Terhune, Jim, 80
Texas Western (Texas-El Paso) Miners, 17, 70, 172, 193-194, 224, 232
Texas Western Miners, 193-194, 232
Thompson, John, 111
Thomson, Bobby, 199
Timberlake, Aminu, 206

INDEX

Townes, Garland, 238-239
Tsioropoulos, Louis, 240
Tulsa Golden Hurricane, 28, 86, 150
Turner, Wayne, 42, 243-244
Turpin, Melvin, 39
Twin Towers, 203

U

UCLA Bruins, 20, 22, 104, 140, 173, 219
Unbelievables, 180
Unforgettables, 26, 40, 83, 218
Untouchables, 180
U.S. Basketball Writers Association, 124
U.S. News and World Report, 95
U.S. Olympic Basketball Team, 167, 227
U.S. Olympic Trials, 56, 130

USA Today, 109, 151, 246-247
Utah Utes, 147, 166, 190

V

Vanderbilt Commodores, 132, 136, 183, 234
Vaughan, Claude, 96-97
Vaught, Jamie H., 36, 76, 81, 95, 109, 124, 143
Vecsey, Peter, 109

W

Walker, Antoine, 29, 84-85, 243
Walker, Kenny, 81
Walker, Owen, 217
Wallace, Tom, 68, 81, 85, 155, 247
Walsh, Matt, 208
Walters, La Donna, 220
Walton, Bill, 140
Watson, Bobby, 240

Wembley Stadium, 129, 131
West, Jerry, 72, 81
Wheeler, Lonnie, 18-19
Whitaker, Lucian, 240
Wieberg, Steve, 151
Wiggins, Bill, 216
Williams, LaVon, 242
Windsor, Bob, 36
Wojciechowski, Steve, 42
Wolff, Alexander, 82, 123
Wooden, John, 20, 104, 111, 173
Woods, Mark, 147-148, 176, 199-200, 207, 234, 245
Woods, Sean, 26
World Series, 199
Worthy, James, 84

Y

Yates, George, 54

Other books in the
Golden Ages of College Sports
series by Wilton Sharpe

BULLDOG
MADNESS
Great Eras in
Georgia Football

BUCKEYE
MADNESS
Great Eras in
Ohio State Football

TAR HEEL
MADNESS
Great Eras in
North Carolina Basketball

Watch for these titles coming in 2006:

LONGHORN
MADNESS
Great Eras in
Texas Football

FIGHTING IRISH
MADNESS
Great Eras in
Notre Dame Football